D1564681

Labor Relations in Education

Policies, Politics, and Practices

Todd A. DeMitchell

Published in partnership with the
Association of School Business Officials International

ROWMAN & LITTLEFIELD EDUCATION

A division of

ROWMAN & LITTLEFIELD PUBLISHERS, INC.
Lanham • New York • Toronto • Plymouth, UK

Published in partnership with the
Association of School Business Officials International

Published in the United States of America
by Rowman & Littlefield Education
A Division of Rowman & Littlefield Publishers, Inc.
A wholly owned subsidiary of The Rowman & Littlefield Publishing Group, Inc.
4501 Forbes Boulevard, Suite 200, Lanham, Maryland 20706
www.rowmaneducation.com

Estover Road
Plymouth PL6 7PY
United Kingdom

British Library Cataloguing in Publication Information Available

Library of Congress Cataloging-in-Publication Data

DeMitchell, Todd A.
    Labor relations in education : policies, politics, and practices / Todd A. DeMitchell.
        p. cm.
    "Published in partnership with the Association of School Business Officials
International."
    ISBN 978-1-60709-583-5 (cloth : alk. paper) — ISBN 978-1-60709-584-2 (pbk. : alk.
paper) — ISBN 978-1-60709-585-9 (electronic)
    1. Collective labor agreements—Education, Higher—United States. 2. Collective
bargaining—Education—United States. I. Association of School Business Officials
International. II. Title.
    LB2335.875.U6D46 2010
    331.89'041371100973—dc22   2009031843

Printed in the United States of America

Contents

Acknowledgments

I wish to thank my father, Bill DeMitchell, for his insight into collective bargaining as well as into life. He was the chief spokesperson for the classified employees in a high school district in Southern California. He first introduced me to the importance of trust and integrity as well as bargaining hard to represent your constituency. His help over the years is deeply appreciated.

And, I always acknowledge Terri, my wife, and the central role that she has in my life.

Chapter 1

Introduction

We have not been able to achieve all that we had hoped for through the collective bargaining process, and it is time to do something additional and different.

—Al Shanker, 1985[1]

In the last fifty-plus years teacher unions have impacted the governance of America's public schools. The two teacher unions have become major policy and political players not only at the local school district level, but also at the national level. In those states that have public sector collective bargaining laws, governance has become bilateral on issues of wages, benefits, and terms and conditions of employment. As educators pursue reform strategies, those strategies must also come to the bargaining table because real reform impacts terms and conditions of employment.

Understanding unions, their history and their work, is important for effective school stewardship. This is true for all educators. Administrators must work with unions, and teachers work in a collective bargaining environment and need to understand how their union works and what a collective bargaining environment means to their professional practice.[2]

This book focuses on the policies and laws that gave rise to public sector bargaining, the politics that accompany the competition for scarce resources—who gets what?—and the practices of bargaining and managing a contract. The eight chapters are divided into three sections with a look to the future, Chapter 8, and a glossary of terms, Chapter 9.

The first chapter of the section Policies, "Labor Relations in Education," explores the work of unions, the policies/contracts that are the outcome of their work, and how the contract formalizes, and standardizes relationships.

1

The next chapter, Chapter Three, "The Legal Framework," focuses on the history of teacher unions, their relationship to the National Labor Relations Act and the resulting industrial labor relations model for public sector collective bargaining, and the retrenchment of public unionism.

The second section, Politics, has three chapters. The fourth chapter, "Community and Conflict," casts collective bargaining within the political atmosphere of competing interests. Chapter 5 reviews the conundrum of being a member of a profession and being a member of a union—the issue of whether the organization is called an association or a union underscores this paradox. Teachers may want to be seen as members of a profession/association, but may be willing to engage in union activities (strikes, work to rule,[3] etc.) to achieve their self-interests? Chapter 6 discusses how policies of reform fare at the bargaining table. Judith Warren Little underscores the importance of this topic writing that there is scant knowledge about the "relative salience of the union compared with other sources in shaping teachers' response to or involvement in reform initiatives."[4]

The third section is Practices. This section includes Chapter 7, "Preparation and Practice: At the Table." It provides the context for what happens at the table and suggestions for how to prepare for bargaining.

A full simulation, the Arroyo Wells School District Simulation, is included in the Appendix.[5] I developed and use this simulation in my public sector collective bargaining course. The simulation begins with all students being placed on either the management or labor bargaining team. They learn to work together in their teams developing proposals and strategies to further the interests of their constituency, the union members or the school district. I conclude the course with ten hours of expedited bargaining.

I have provided all of the backup materials that I use in the simulation. They are found in Appendix A numbers one through thirteen. Normally I do not provide these backup materials. This allows the students to figure what information they do not have that they need in order to craft proposals. This is not possible in this format. However, I do encourage the students to go through the process of analyzing what information is needed but not available. This will add to the real world skills that are necessary to bargain effectively.

In addition, I have provided a statement of bargaining interests for both bargaining teams to use as a guide in preparing for bargaining. Appendix B has the interest letter for management and Appendix C has the interest letter for the union. There is no effective way to keep the contents of the interest letters secret; interests of the parties will come out in the negotiation process, but I request that the bargaining parties refrain from reading the other's interest letters.

Throughout the book I consistently use the terms union and management. These are terms that are used in private sector labor relations. I do not specifically discuss public sector unions that include custodians, clerks, secretaries, bus drivers, or maintenance workers. This does not mean that these unions and the labor relations that characterize those employees are not important—they are important. But I have limited space. The public sector collective bargain laws that pertain to teachers also pertain to other unions in a school district including administrator unions, which I will not be able to discuss as well.

I approach labor relations using *Getting Together*[6] and *Getting to Yes*[7] as conceptual frameworks. Consequently, the focus is not on just getting a contract. The success of bargaining is not predicated upon signing the contract. Success is determined by whether the labor relations, employee/employer relations are enhanced and improved or at a minimum not harmed. Bargaining is not a success if one side or the other is angry at the end of bargaining and has a score to settle in the next round. Fisher and Brown in *Getting Together* write, "If we don't feel positive after the last transaction, we may dread the next and have more difficulty dealing with it."[8] Collective bargaining that does not solve problems, but rather creates or perpetuates them, cannot be considered successful just because two reluctant or angry parties signed the last page of the contract.

I view collective bargaining as a reel of film. One end is blank waiting to be imprinted. The other is the history of the working relations of the educators, teachers and administrators, union and management. Consequently, bargaining is not an unconnected event; it is part of the reel of labor relations. The bargaining of a contract is tied to the past and helps to structure the future.

What happens at the table, how the participants treat each other has consequences for the present and for the future. Administrator trashing and union bashing at the table spills over to the schools and the relations outside of the table. This leaves the public with the perception that the callous and inept are lead by the indifferent and incompetent. Public education loses its public in this situation.

It is my hope that this book will help to build a knowledge base about unions and collective bargaining, provide some practical suggestions about bargaining, and give the opportunity to learn about bargaining by taking part in a simulation that leads to improved labor relations between educators. As I stated above, signing a contract is not the measure of the success of collective bargaining. The measure of success is whether the relationship in this people-intensive activity of teaching has been strengthened or harmed.

NOTES

1. Thomas Toch, *In the Name of Excellence: The Struggle to Reform the Nation's Schools, Why it's Failing, and What Should be Done* (New York: Oxford University Press,1991), 134.

2. Steve Farkas, Jean Johnson, and Ann Duffett, *Stand By Me: What Teachers Really Think About Unions, Merit Pay, and Other Professional Matters* (New York: Public Agenda, 2003), 18. Teachers appear to have a "limited level engagement with their unions."

3. An example of the conflict between professional responsibility and hardball union activity such as work to rule is found in Newton, Massachusetts in 1992. The teachers voted to work to rule during difficult contract negotiations. The work to rule prevented teachers from meeting with parents after school hours and some refused to write letters of recommendation for college-bound students.

Todd A. DeMitchell and Richard Fossey, *The Limits of Law-Based School Reform: Vain Hopes and False Promises* (Lancaster, PA: Technomic Publishing Co. Inc., 1997), 44.

4. Judith Warren Little, "Teachers' Professional Development in a Climate of Educational Reform," *Educational Evaluation and Policy Analysis* 15, 129–151 (1993): 146.

5. Student course evaluation comments on the simulation include: "The simulation is a well-tuned tool for promoting our learning." "The simulation was invaluable for the experience of negotiations." "The simulation at the end was an excellent lab in which to experiment with our newly learned skills."

6. Roger Fisher and Scott Brown, *Getting Together: Building Relationships As We Negotiate* (New York: Penguin Books, 1988)

7. Roger Fisher and William Ury, *Getting to Yes: Negotiating Agreement Without Giving In.* New York: Penguin Books, (1981)

8. Fisher and Brown, *supra* note 6, p. 8.

Section I

Policies

Chapter 2

Labor Relations in Education

> Unions, like any organization, will not survive if they do not serve the needs of their members. But unions will not survive and grow, if they only serve the needs of their members.[1]

The term labor relations, for many, invokes an image of factory assembly lines, coalmines, longshoreman, and truckers. This is on the mark because the roots of the term labor relations are found in the relationship between unions and employers, and the early relations between employer and worker focused on these industrial work settings. Industrial relations systems consist of rules that govern work, the worker and the workplace.[2] Cresswell and Murphy consider labor relations as complex, because the "defining of employee-employer relations is continuous."[3] The relationship is always in process being formed and reformed building on the past by both parties—the reel of film.

There are three classes of actors in industrial relations: the managers/administrators, the representatives who speak for labor (the union), and the third parties who establish and regulate the system (Public Labor Relations Board in New Hampshire and the Public Employee Relations Board in California, for example).[4] Individuals who work in the field of labor relations negotiate contracts, including compensation rates, benefits, working conditions, and rates of advancement, between workers and managers and manage those contracts.

Labor relations are not just confined to the traditional private sector union workplace of the factory floor or the mine. Starting in the latter half of the twentieth century many public employees joined their unionized brethren who had made great strides in organizing starting in the 1930s. This boost was given to public employees when President John F. Kennedy signed Executive Order 10988 allowing federal public employees to bargain. Only

Wisconsin had allowed its public employees to bargain when President Kennedy signed the order in 1962.[5] Public education became one of those unionized public work settings.

Another key event in the development of collective bargaining in public education was the New York teachers' strike of April 11, 1962 in which more than half of the teachers walked the picket line. Kerchner and Mitchell consider the outcome of the strike as causing "a permanent change in the relationship between teachers and their school district employers."[6] A profession used the hardball tactics of the industrial union to further the self-interests of its members. Teachers came together, took a stand, and changed the educational landscape.

Education today is a heavily unionized workforce, possibly the most heavily unionized in the nation. Consequently, "[t]eacher unions are major participants in American educational practice."[7] The National Education Association (NEA), the nation's largest teachers union, has about 3.2 million members working in pre-school settings to higher education.[8] The American Federation of Teachers (AFT), the second largest teachers union, has about 1.4 million members in 3,000 local chapters and is an affiliated international union of the AFL-CIO.[9] Rural, suburban, and urban schools have unionized faculty. Recently, a unionized faculty is arising in charter schools; a reform predicated upon reducing the hold of legal mechanisms including collective bargaining agreements.[10]

The NEA and AFT grew from different traditions, which initially shaped their approach to unionization and collective bargaining. In its early years, NEA was considered a professional organization and was not dominated by classroom teachers. Rather its leadership tended to be superintendents, college presidents, and college professors. In contrast, AFT, from its inception, has seen itself as a teachers' union. "It was organized by teachers, the membership was composed of teachers, and most important, the leadership came from classroom teachers."[11]

The emergence of AFT in the 1960s forced NEA to shift its focus more strongly toward teachers' bread-and-butter interests. Today, differences between the nation's two largest unions have faded, and both AFT and NEA now clearly see themselves as advocates and representatives of classroom teachers. However, their convergence of goals does not obscure the fact that not all teachers are ardent supporters of the unionization of the profession.[12]

Some have argued that the NEA despite its early roots and the AFT because of its early roots, have embraced the tradition of the factory floor and the inferno like steel mills giving teachers the feel of the classic blue-collar worker "where winning workers big checks for the shortest possible hours has been the aim and quality of product is considered management's worry."[13] But, many teachers "simply believe that their unions protect their interests."[14] In a nationwide survey of teachers, 81 percent believe that their working conditions and salaries would be much worse without their unions bargaining collectively for them, even though about two thirds aren't involved in their union.[15]

Wirt and Kirst assert that no other group has had "increased influence on education policy in recent decades as much as have teachers. The timid rabbits of 30 years ago are today's ravening tigers in the jungle of school systems."[16]

In recent years, both major teachers unions have become powerful participants in the nation's educational policy debates where they make their voices heard regarding the interests of teachers and teachers' views about educational practice. They have a powerful voice in debates over policy and practice. In some cases, the power of the union becomes part of the election in which one party candidate seeks their endorsement and another decries their endorsement and involvement in public affairs.

For example, the general election in 2008 saw "teachers' unions around the country [shift] into high gear in the countdown to the presidential election. . . ."[17] Candidates often court individual teachers by separating them from their union; a common refrain is "I support teachers, my concern is with the union which is hurting education." This occurs in public elections at the national, state, and local levels. Hess and Leal found that unions were the leading interest group in school board politics.[18]

Separating teachers from their union on the political stage also occurs over legislation. For example, the Governor of Michigan was pushing for educational reform that impacted the union and its policy positions on education. The Governor drew a distinction between teachers and their union. A member of the state board of education explained the strategy as avoiding the charge of teacher bashing and casting the political tensions as a struggle over power with the union concerned with promoting its political and economic power.[19] Attacking teachers as a profession is often a losing political strategy, while portraying the union as protecting the status quo in the face of needed change often gains political capital for its adherent.

At the time that unions gained influence over public education, the education reform movement grew and intensified. Questions have arisen with regard to whether teachers unions can be effective promoters of educational reform while maintaining their traditional role as assertive advocates on the bread-and-butter issues important to their members. Unions stand in the way of reform and the achievement of basic bread-and-butter items is a necessary condition of reform are two opposite responses to the role of unions as our educational system pursues reform strategies.

The influence of unions and collective bargaining on the operations of school districts is demonstrated in a front-page, above the fold article in the *Boston*

Globe, which reads, "City braces for a one-day school strike."[20] The newspaper provided a guide for parents in the event of a school strike. And, in Miami-Dade County, Florida, the United Teachers of Dade, an affiliate of the AFT crafted an" unlikely" partnership with the private education firm, Edison Schools Inc., to build and manage ten charter schools.[21] Unions, particularly teacher unions, exert influence over public education, which needs to be a topic of study. I have taught collective bargaining for almost two decades, I am always surprised at how little, beginning teachers, experienced classroom teachers, and beginning school administrators know about collective bargaining and the role of unions.

Because of the influential role that unions play and the major activity of a union is collective bargaining, labor relations in education is an important part of a school leader's role. A majority of the states have public sector collective bargaining laws. Therefore, understanding unions and their work is important for effective school stewardship and union leadership. Knowledge of the dimensions of a contract, how to bargain it, and how to manage it enable educational leaders to lead and improve their organizations, schools and unions.

Negotiating the contract is a major part of labor relations. The other major part is managing the contract. While specialists, sometimes hired guns from the outside, are often tasked with negotiating the contract, all administrators in the school district are responsible for managing the contract. Labor relations are part of the larger human resource function. Young and Castetter write that the goals of human resources are to "attract, select, induct, develop, retain, and motivate personnel to achieve the system's mission; maximize career opportunities for employees; and coordinate organizational and individual objectives."[22] Negotiating and managing a contract impacts these human resource goals. Quality labor relations attract and retain employees.

Fifty years of bargaining in the schools, and the rise of the two major teacher unions and their role as major policy actors underscores the need for understanding labor relations in education. This chapter will explore the work of unions and collective bargaining. But, first we begin with the role of people in education because it is unlike many industrial union workplaces in which technology is an extension of the worker. Education is work delivered individual-to-individual, even in a virtual school.

EDUCATION: A PEOPLE INTENSIVE ENTERPRISE

Schooling is a social experience. A teacher's workspace is unique as is the work setting. It is far removed from the routinized, and in some cases, robot dominated factory floor and the workspace of other adults. Teachers have a large degree of autonomy within the confines of their classroom walls and primarily work with groups of children. Teachers are both isolated and protected from other educators and outside influences. Their work is delivered in an intensely personal environment. While teachers do not create the physical space, they are largely responsible for the creation of the environment in which instruction is delivered and learning takes place.

In fact, this is a recognized part of the teacher's professional responsibilities. The linchpin of our system of education is the teacher in his or her classroom exercising a large amount of discretion as to how that classroom is run and how knowledge is imparted and skills taught. In effect, teachers are decision makers and not just decision implementers.[23]

Teachers stand at the core of schooling. From this simple beginning the labor relations that take place in public schools is structured by the delivery system of labor, which is intensely personal. Students refer to "my" teacher, and teachers discuss their class in terms of "their" students. It is within this personal setting where teachers are largely separated from other adults, and they, to borrow from Hiam Ginott, "create the weather"[24] in their classrooms that the structures of labor relations with its collectively bargained and standard agreement plays out.

Susan Moore Johnson in her early study of teacher unions states,

> it is individuals who strike bargains, make concessions, interpret language, advise strategies, and act on the basis of what they think others will do. Typically, personalities predominate over roles, rules and rituals. Collective bargaining is a people-centered process, just as schools are people-centered places.[25]

WHAT DO UNIONS DO?

What are unions? According to Tannenbaum "unions are organizations designed to protect and enhance the social and economic welfare of their members."[26] A union is "a continuous association of wage earners for the purpose of maintaining or improving the conditions of their working lives."[27] Lieberman asserts that a union "exists in whole or in part to represent employees to their employers on their terms and conditions of employment."[28] McDonnell and Pascal characterize the role of unions in the following manner: first, they operate as political interest groups, working to obtain benefits from the external environment, and, second they also function as voluntary organizations that must meet members' demands in the type and level of benefits they obtain and the services they provide. The challenge for the unions is to obtain sufficient benefits to maintain their membership, while also operating effectively in a world of political bargaining and compromise.[29]

In 1990, NEA's newly installed president stated, "As a union, we have to be in the forefront of the kinds of funding that are needed at the federal, state, and local levels."[30] Unions lobby and try to exert influence on political bodies to gain desired benefits or thwart perceived undesirable consequences to their institutional goals. In many ways they are just like other external educational special interest groups, such as school board associations, tax payer watchdog groups, and fundamental Christian organizations, that vie for their place on the public agenda. Thus, the union's voice is part of the cacophony of voices struggling to be heard by lawmakers. However, unions are also inside players as well as outside players in the school district's policy arena.

Teacher unions as political interest groups provide visibility upon the national, regional, and local stages. They have an influential role as seen by the political candidates at all levels who either court their support or use the teacher unions as the whipping boy for the challenges public education faces and the failures it and its students have suffered. Education is an important, if not one of the most important, activities of government.[31]

Elections provide an opportunity for teacher unions and other interest groups to influence curriculum, assessment, and accountability. In the 2008 general election the federal, systems changing legislation No Child Left Behind (NCLB) became part of the policy debate. The NEA, which is highly critical of the federal law at the national and state level, backed candidates who held a similar position.[32] While the NEA tended to back Democrats who were critical of NCLB it also backed Republicans who supported other union positions.[33]

As an organization, unions sell a service to specific groups of employees. Since unions can and must compete for membership, this is especially true in education, with the NEA and AFT seeking to be the exclusive representative, they must be able to demonstrate that its members receive a value for the dues they pay for the union to represent them. A major activity of unions is bargaining with management over the wages, benefits, terms, and conditions of employment and then managing the contract for consistent, uniform compliance across the school district. Their traditional duty is to meet members' demands in the type and level of benefits sought from the employer.

Potential consumers of union service judge the value received by what is secured through bargaining and other activities, which enhance the security of the employee. Essentially, unions try to get better wages, benefits, and working conditions for its members than they could get on their own. Unions speak for the employee to the employer on those three items. In addition, the union represents the employee's interests and rights regarding job security whether it involves discipline, layoffs, or dismissal. In fact, in most schools that have a collective bargaining agreement, a teacher has the right to have a union representative present in meeting with the school administrators in which discipline is a likely outcome.

Teachers join a union in order to secure more tangible benefits than they would get without the union. If the union cannot secure an appropriate increase in wages, health care insurance, sick leave benefits, and other such benefits, why should the teacher pay money to join? The union must provide a service that the teachers believe they could not gain on their own. The union must deliver on bread-and-butter issues as well as providing job security. Otherwise, the union is nothing more than a social club, nice to join for the camaraderie and professional stimulation, but not essential for the economic survival of its members.

Once a union has been elected by a majority of the members who would form the bargaining unit, the union becomes their exclusive representative. Only that union can speak for the members of the bargaining unit. The union and the school board sign any contract that is subsequently negotiated. Because the union has the exclusive voice representing teachers' resolutions of grievances, overall enforcement of the contract, and any changes to the contract are done by the union. Individual teachers gave up their right to bargain for themselves over their wages, benefits, and terms and conditions of employment. In many ways, prior to collective bargaining management spoke for individual teachers. With collective bargaining their union speaks for individual teachers. However, teachers have greater influence over their union through the elections of union officers.

In recent years, both major teachers unions have become powerful participants in the nation's educational policy debates, where they make their voices heard regarding the interests of teachers and teachers' views about educational practice. School leaders face the challenge of learning how to work effectively in a unionized environment in which teacher rights are codified in an enforceable contract. Teachers face the challenge of understanding how the contract affects their daily work. Union representatives face the challenge of shoring up support among their teachers for the work of the union;[34] "teachers may not see unions and collective bargaining as being related to activities that are at the core of teaching."[35] However, it is a foolish administrator who assumes that teachers will not publicly support their union. Horizontal pressure is powerful, at least as powerful as vertical pressure in many situations.

WHAT IS COLLECTIVE BARGAINING?

First, why does collective bargaining matter? "Though they have attracted little media or, until recently, scholarly attention, teacher collective bargaining agreements shape nearly everything public schools do."[36] "Teachers stand at the crossroads of education. Educational leaders can get nothing done of any lasting value except through the efforts of teachers."[37]

Since collective bargaining affects terms and conditions of employment—the work of teachers—what is bargained and how it is bargained is important. Bargaining at its best "is a legitimate vehicle for problem solving."[38] While it has the ability to set parties against each other when there is a conflict of interests, it also has the ability to bring parties together for meaningful discussions. A collective bargaining agreement is essentially a contract in which both parties agree to the services that teachers will provide the terms and conditions of employment, the wages, and benefits exchanged for the services.

Collective bargaining is probably the major work of unions. It clearly is the most visible work of unions in school districts. "In collective bargaining, the union is usually the driving force, and its performance in this mode is ordinarily the crucial test of its value to the employees it represents."[39] A union's stance on policy issues may garner the attention of the media and the public, but the work of unions from its members' perspective is bargaining, implementing, and enforcing a contract. The union is judged by how well it does its work.

Collective bargaining moved three critical decisions from the unilateral decision making of school boards to bilateral decision making. Prior to unions gaining the right to bargain as the exclusive representative of its members, the employer could make unilateral decisions regarding employment. With collective bargaining, decisions affecting the wages, benefits, terms and conditions of employment must be bargained. They are considered mandatory subjects of bargaining. For example, the number of instructional periods that a teacher must teach each day is a term and condition of employment, which must be bargained.[40]

Another category of bargainable items is permissive subjects of bargaining. States regulate the labor contract and labor relations through legislation "but leave the remainder of the teacher's labor contract unspecified."[41] It is this unspecified portion that often forms the subjects that are permissive. While the failure to bargain over a mandatory subject of bargaining gives rise to a legal proceeding called an unfair labor practice (ULP), neither a school district nor a union are required to bargain over a permissive subject of bargaining.

A permissive subject of bargaining may be raised at the table by one of the parties, typically the union, but the other party can decide that it does or does not want to include the subject in the contract. Neither party "can insist upon such subjects as a condition of executing a contract."[42] In other words, a party cannot insist to impasse that the other party agree on the permissive subject of bargaining.[43] If a party does not want to bargain a subject that is permissible, the part need only say no. It is wise, however, to provide a rationale for the "no" so as to keep getting to "yes."

These topics may vary from state to state. For example, in some states class size is considered a permissive subject of bargaining. A school district that decides to bargain a permissive subject of bargaining must approach this decision with caution. Once the subject is in the contract, it will remain in the contract until it is bargained out of the contract. Most of the time school districts do not want to expand the subjects that they must bargain.

The third type of bargaining is prohibited. A prohibited subject of bargaining cannot be bargained. For example, in New Hampshire, a collective bargaining agreement cannot contain a provision that gives a non-tenured teacher a due process hearing right for a non-renomination decision. Prohibited subjects of bargaining are usually policy issues. Prohibiting the bargaining of policy keeps policy making an essential public responsibility that cannot be bargained away. School boards are elected by the public and are responsible to the public via the ballot box. Giving unions the ability to bargain policy removes the public from the policy making process because unions are not directly accountable to the public, it is argued.

The Supreme Court of New Jersey in *Ridgefield Park Education Association v. Ridgefield Park Board of Education* buttressed this idea of union separation from public policy formation when it wrote: "[T]he very foundation of representative democracy would be endangered if decisions of significant matters of governmental policy were left to the process of collective negotiations, where citizen participation is precluded."[44] Since policy initiatives are placed by law in the hands of management, the faculty role is reduced to reaction and response in a collective bargaining environment.

FORMALIZE, STANDARDIZE, AND CENTRALIZE RELATIONS

Collective bargaining has three results that impact labor relations in a school district. First, the contract formalizes relationships between teachers and administrators. Second, it standardizes teachers' work because the contract defines the working conditions for all teachers who serve under the contract. And, third it centralizes relationships in that standardization is best assured when the two parties to the contract collaborate to ensure that the contract is applied equitably to all members of the unit. Collective bargaining is a rule making activity. The duty of the enforcement of the rules belongs to both parties, management and the union, thus centralizing decision making.

Formalization, standardization, and centralization typically occur because, as a matter of social policy, collective bargaining is designed to achieve labor peace. Labor peace is more easily maintained and managed if it is controlled. Formalizing, standardizing, and centralizing relationships are means that are used to attain labor peace, manage conflict, and maintain stable operations. Each of these three effects on in labor relations in education resulting from collective bargaining will be discussed below.

Formalize Relationships

Prior to collective bargaining relations between teachers and principals could be informal. With the advent of collective bargaining the relationship between employee and supervisory, teacher and principal, is no longer just between those two. Their interaction is now connected to others in a larger mosaic.

Reducing the relationship to a written contract that in many school districts is literally reduced to a size that could fit in a pocket, helped to formalize the relationships. Comments such as, "I have to check on the contract before we proceed further" catches educators in a "web of rules." The contract becomes a mediating force between teacher and principal. Individual responses to specific needs are often replaced with a response that fits within the contract. A tug on one strand of the web of rules can be felt through out the web. What happens between one teacher and principal can affect all.

This is not to say that collective bargaining does not allow for the give-and-take that characterizes a good workplace or good school. Those informal relationships still exist. But, lurking behind the space for informal, collegial relationships carved out from the *us* and *them* industrial union mindset is the knowledge that informality will give way to formality if the contract is threatened. It is my view that true collaboration grows from informal relations more than formal relations. Cooperation, which is different and sometimes mistaken for collaboration, can work in a formalized atmosphere. Adam Urbanski, a nationally known union leader, writes, "Central to any specific efforts to improve our urban schools, is the relationship between school managers and teachers' unions. Without labor management collaboration, even the best efforts of management are tantamount to one hand clapping."[45]

It can be argued that a more formal relationship grounded in the bilateral contract establishes a more professional relationship, one not based on personal relationships conjuring up the specter of favoritism. A formal relationship better characterizes the hierarchical reality of large school districts, some could argue.

Standardize Relationships

Through collective bargaining, "unions tend to 'standardize' the workplace."[46] This has consequences for education. Carini writes, because the union contract applies equally to all teachers in all schools within the school district, contracts tend to "produce more standardized work environments."[47] The standardized work environment envisioned in a contract fails to capture the ethos of the education profession, the complexity of teaching, or the need for some autonomy in the classroom in order to effectively respond to the needs of students. Cooper and Liotta describe teaching as "highly interpersonal, individualistic, and human."[48] These are not the attributes/activities that are easily standardized so as to enhance control and enforcement.

Standardization is not the same as professional standards developed through rigorous examination of practice, which comports with the accepted literature that forms the core knowledge of the profession. A basic tenet of collective bargaining and unionization is that the negotiated contract must apply uniformly and equally to all teachers covered by the contract. How the contract is interpreted and applied in one school must be consistent with how it is interpreted and applied in all schools in the district.

A uniform contract calls for standard application irrespective of differing conditions and needs at the various schools. "Under conventional labor relations, unions negotiate for an entire district but pay little heed to the needs of individual schools."[49] Standard cookie cutter responses replace hand-crafted responses in a uniform contract. This standardization and resulting uniformity do not fit easily into a profession that requires flexibility of response to context. The predictability of the factory line arguably does not capture the richness, autonomy, and interdependence of the classroom. Collegiality and pedagogical technique necessary to education do not blend easily into the structures of contract language.[50] Normative descriptions of professional work do not easily translate into the legal descriptions of a contract.

Professional teaching practice calls for diagnosis of the situational factors of the class and its individual students and an adaptation of strategies. Professional practice demands flexibility and differential action based on the context of the learning situation. In addition, Johnson and Kardos note that teacher collective bargaining has "meant more standardized schools, leaving principals with less latitude to run their schools."[51] Unfortunately, the standard union work rules found in contracts too often contribute to an inflexible environment.

Karl E. Weick has characterized schools as loosely coupled organizations.[52] Loosely coupled organizations are characterized as largely self-functioning subsystems. They often have a lack of coordination. For example, prior to No Child Left Behind (NCLB), if one asked a teacher where the school district curriculum guide was located, the query may be met with a blank stare because teachers sought autonomy once their classroom door was closed. A more tightly coupled structure, a top-down structure, is a result of NCLB.

Now teachers not only know where the district's curriculum guide is located but they refer to it as well as the state grade level expectations.

A tradeoff with a more tightly coupled system is that a loosely coupled system is a good system for localized adaptation. Local groups can adapt to their part of the environment without changing the entire system. The opposite, standardization, may be too restrictive. Standardization leads to a more tightly coupled system with a resulting greater control and command over activities. Standardization leads to less flexibility. Since the standardization of a contract impacts teachers and principals primarily, it leads to less flexibility, less ability to adapt quickly to unique conditions and changes in the work environment and new pressures from the external environment.

A quick look at the Detroit teachers' strike in September of 1992 reinforces this conclusion that standardization leads to less flexibility at the school site level. In 1992, the Detroit teachers went on strike. The Detroit strike, in part, was over the school board's conception of restructuring schools so as to give the schools greater autonomy and flexibility to respond to their unique circumstances. "Under the school board proposal at issue in the Detroit strike, a school could become 'empowered' if its principal, 75 percent of its teachers, and its parent council agreed."[53]

An empowered school would be free to operate as it wished, as long it met the achievement standards for Detroit students and it balanced its budget. An empowered school, according to the school board proposal could waive provisions of the teaching contract after a two-week notice to the union of the waiver request. This two week notice would give union leaders time to discuss the issue with the teachers and to possibly convince them to vote against the measure thus preserving the contract for all.

In response to the school board's plan to decentralize and restructure decision making in the school district, John Elliott, the teachers' union president, argued that "Detroit teachers prefer a centralized school system with the same work rules and procedures for everyone."[54] A school board member countered the union's insistence that the same work rules must apply to every teacher that it was to him "the antithesis of professionalism."[55]

Randall Eberts et al. draw an interesting intersection between the standardizing affect of the negotiated contract with student outcomes and drop out rates. They cite studies that found modestly positive effects of teacher unions for average students but negative effects for atypical students.[56] They posit that part of the answer is the "standardizing effect of teacher unions on schools."[57] Their explanation for this phenomenon is that unionized schools rely more heavily on traditional instruction, which benefits the average student, rather than on differentiated instruction, which benefits the atypical student.

DeMitchell and Cobb, in their study of teacher perceptions of professionalism and unionism, offer another view of the role of the standardizing effect of the contract on teaching. They asked whether quality teaching can be standardized into a contract. The responding teachers cast doubt on the relationship. On a Likert type scale of one strongly disagree to five strongly agree, the teachers had a mean of 2.45 tending to the "Disagree" (point 2 on the scale) that quality teaching can be standardized into a contract. Only 16.7 percent of the responding teachers "Agreed" or "Strongly Agreed" with the proposition, whereas, 62.8 percent "Disagreed" or "Strongly Disagreed" with whether quality teaching can be standardized into a contract.[58]

The core professional activity of teachers, teaching, according to these respondents, cannot be successfully bargained into a contract. The contract, with its standardizing effect, cannot capture the uniqueness of teaching.

The Mayor of Boston commissioned a report on the implementation of school-based management reform. School-based management requires a decentralization of authority. This reform strategy was designed to give teachers and principals more authority to run their individual schools. In return for increased authority and increased salaries, teachers promised to become more accountable for educational results.

Fossey and Miles concluded in their report to Mayor "that school-based management had little impact on the quality of education in Boston."[59] The study identified two major reasons why school-based management had so little effect on school performance. First, the School Committee and the administrators lacked commitment to the reform as evidenced by their reluctance to grant waivers and a seeming unwillingness to cede authority to individual schools. The second reason, and most important one for this study, was the relationship between the union and the administration reflected in the union contract, grievances, and arbitration decisions.

Specifically, the study pointed to contract rules that contributed to an inflexible environment for managing schools, an emphasis on seniority, and an industrial model of labor relations that "discouraged innovation by requiring that all changes in working conditions be submitted to the union for negotiation prior to implementation."[60] These were rules that valued standardization throughout the school district in contradiction to the tenets of school-based management that decentralized important decisions.

In other words, the reform of decentralization to move decisions closer to the place where they are enacted conflicted with the standardization required by a collective bargaining agreement. The conundrum of the reform of the decentralization of school-based management in a collective bargaining environment is underscored in that the schools could seek a waiver of the collective bargaining agreement. The standardizing effect of the contract required a waiver for the reform to work.

Centralization

This need for standardization leads to centralization since the contract must be administered uniformly. The contract is between the union and the school board, therefore both parties are charged with its uniform application. Uniformity is enforced at the central office by both union and school district officials through the formal grievance process and the informal and sometimes guarded relationship that often develops between union officials and district level administrators. Both parties to the contract seek uniform application of the contract; otherwise, instability might ensue, thus endangering the labor peace achieved by the contract. "Both the union and the district office administrators seek to centralize and standardize behavior through consistent rule interpretation, scrutiny, and enforcement."[61]

Formalization, standardization, and centralization as a by-product of collective bargaining may not well serve education. Susan Moore Johnson in her early and seminal study of the impact of unions in schools wrote "[t]he increased centralization of the school district is thought by others to have excessively and unwisely formalized, standardized, and rationalized school operations."[62] It is no coincidence that some reforms, such as restructuring schools require a suspension of some of the more inflexible articles in a collective bargaining agreement.[63]

Uniqueness or context of teaching environments is typically not accommodated in collective bargaining agreements. Normative descriptions of professional work do not easily translate into the legal descriptions and standardizing language of a contract. Collegiality and contextualized decision making, important aspects of professional educational practice do not fit neatly into a system that is standardized and centralized.

NOTES

1. Elaine Bernard. *Why Unions Matter.* National Education Association. Site visited February 27, 2001 at http://www.nea.org/publiced/unions/html, 2.

2. Charles J. Coleman, *Managing Labor Relations in the Public Sector* (San Francisco: Jossey-Bass Publishers, 1990), 15.

3. Anthony M. Cresswell and Micahel J. Murphy, *Teachers, Unions, and Collective Bargaining in Public Education* (Berkeley, CA: McCutchan Publishing Corporation, 1980), 385.

4. Coleman, *supra* note 2.

5. Carol Wright and David E. Gundersen. "Unions and Teachers: Differences in the State of the Nation." *Journal of Employment and Labor Law* 10, 1–12 (2004): 2. Site accessed August 16, 2008 at http://homepages.ius.edu/ LCHRISTI/Journal%20of%20emply/Teacher%20Unions-Gundersen.pdf.

6. Charles Taylor Kerchner and Douglas Mitchell, *The Changing Idea of a Teachers' Union* (New York: Falmer Press, 1988) 1–2.

7. Nina Bascia, *Unions in Teachers' Professional Lives: Social, Intellectual, and Practical* (New York: Teachers College Press, 1994) 1.

8. National Education Association. Site visited August 22, 2008 at http://www .nea.org/aboutnea/index.html.

9. American Federation of Teachers. Site visited August 22, 2008 at http://www .aft.org/about/index.htm.

10. Stephen Sawchuck, "Unions Set Sights on High-Profile Charter-Network School," *Education Week*, p. 1, 14–15 (2009). Randi Weingarten, President of the AFT, argued "unionization is a necessity for charter schools' sustained success, once initial enthusiasm wanes and the hard work of educating students sets in" (14).

11. William A. Streshly and Todd A. DeMitchell, *Teacher Unions and TQE: Building Quality Labor Relations* (Thousand Oaks, CA: Corwin Press, Inc, 1994) 9.

12. Jeanne Ponessa, "Alternative Teachers' Groups Highlighted." *Education Week*, (1997) 36. A low-profile, but apparently growing, population of teachers who have declined membership in the country's two major teachers' unions have instead joined local teacher associations" such as the Association of American Educators" (Ibid.).

13. Thomas Toch, "Why Teachers Don't Teach." *U.S. News and World Report*, 62–71 (1996) 64.

14. Steve Farkas, Jean Johnson, and Ann Duffett, *Stand by Me: What Teachers Really Think about Unions, Merit Pay and Other Professional Matters* (Washington, D.C.: Public Agenda, 2003) 17.

15. Ibid.

16. Frederick M. Wirt and Michael W. Kirst, *The Political Dynamics of American Education* (Berkeley, CA: McCuthchan, 1997), 181.

17. Vaishali Honawar, "Unions Battle for Democrats in Swing States," *Education Week*, 1, 14–15 (2008) 1. "By early October [2008], officials said the NEA and its affiliates had distributed more than 4.2 million pieces of mail, made more than 2.1 million phone calls, and sent more than 1.3 million emails to members in battleground states about the Nov. 4 presidential election." 14.

18. Frederick M. Hess and David L. Leal, "School House Politics: Expenditures, Interests, and Competition in School Board Elections." In William Howell (Ed.) *Beseiged: School Boards and the Future of Education Politics* (Washington, D.C.: Brookings Institution Press, 2005) 228–253.

19. William Lowe Boyd, David N. Plank, and Gary Sykes, "Teacher Unions in Hard Times." In Tom Loveless (Ed.) *Conflicting Missions? Teacher Unions and Educational Reform* (Washington, D.C.: Brookings Institution Press 174–210, 2000), 181.

20. Matt Viser. (February 13, 2007). "City braces for a one-day school strike." *Boston Globe*, p. A1–A7.

21. Mark Walsh, "Miami-Dade Teachers' Union Partners With Edison on Charter Plan." *Education Week* (September 20, 2000), 5.

22. I. Phillip Young and William B. Castetter, *The Human Resource Function in Educational Administration (8th Ed.)* (Upper Saddle River, NJ: Pearson, 2004), 4.

23. Samuel B. Bacharach, Joseph B. Shedd, and Sharon C. Conley "School Management and Teacher Unions," *Teachers College Record* 91, 97–114 (1989): 101.

24. Hiam G. Ginott, *Teacher and Child: A Book for Parents and Teachers* (New York: Avon, 1972). "I am the decisive element in the classroom. It is my personal approach that creates the climate. It is my daily mood that makes the weather. As a teacher I possess tremendous power to make a child's life miserable or joyous. I can be a tool of torture or an instrument of inspiration. I can humiliate or humor, hurt or heal. In all situations it is my response that decides whether a crisis will be escalated or de-escalated, and a child humanized or de-humanized" (xii).

25. Susan Moore Johnson, *Teachers Unions in Schools* (Philadelphia: Temple University Press, 1984) 167–168.

26. Arnold S. Tannenbaum, "Unions." In James G. March, (Ed.) *Handbook of Organizations* (Chicago: Rand McNally and Co., (1965) 705.

27. Sidney Webb and Beatrice Webb, *The History of Trade Unionism (2nd Ed.)*. (New York: Longmans, Green and Company, 1896), 1. Site accessed February 19, 2008 at http://books.google.com/books?id=roAZAAAAMAAJanddq= %22history+of+trade+unionism%22andpg=PP1andots=OsRvhvIr2landsig= U94tPbgqs8XDiLOqKWiyLDEJej4andhl=enandprev=http://www.google.com/sea rch?client=safariandrls=en-usandq=%22History+of+Trade+Unionism%22andie= UTF-8andoe=UTF-8andsa=Xandoi=printandct=titleandcad=one-book-with -thumbnail#PPR3,M1

28. Myron Lieberman, *The Teacher Unions: How the NEA and the AFT Sabotage Reform and Hold Students, Parents, and Taxpayers Hostage to Bureaucracy* (New York: Free Press, 1997), 9.

29. Lorraine M. McDonnell and Anthony Pascal, *Teacher Unions and Educational Reform* (Sanata Monica, CA: RAND, 1988), VII.

30. C. Herrington, NEA's new president: Perspectives on the union's role for the nineties. *Politics of Education Bulletin*, 17 (Winter 1990-91): 2.

31. "Today, education is perhaps the most important function of state and local governments . . . . In these days, it is doubtful that any child may reasonably be expected to succeed in life if he [or she] is denied the opportunity of an education. Such an opportunity, where the state has undertaken to provide it, is a right, which must be made available to all on equal terms." *Brown v. Board of Education*, 347 U.S. 484, 491(1954).

32. Alyson Klein, "Races for Congress Have Sparse Debates on Education Issues." *Education Week* (October 29, 2008): 18–20.

33. Ibid. The NEA supported a Republican over a Democrat in a Congressional election in Washington. The democrat supported merit pay and the republican did not.

34. For example, teachers appear to have a "limited level of engagement with their unions." Farkas, et al., *supra* note 14, p. 18.

35. Todd A. DeMitchell and Richard M. Barton, Collective bargaining and its impact on local educational reform efforts. *Educational Policy* 10, 366–378 (1996): 376.

36. Frederick M. Hess and Martin R. West. *A Better Bargain: Overhauling Teacher Collective Bargaining for the 21st Century* (Cambridge, MA: Harvard University, Program on Education Policy and Governance, n.d.), 9.

37. Todd A. DeMitchell, "Unions, Collective Bargaining, and the Challenges of Leading." In Fenwick W. English (Ed.) *The Sage Handbook of Educational Leadership: Advances in Theory, Research, and Practice* (Thousand Oaks, CA: Sage Publications, 2005), 538–549.

38. William G. Keane, *Win Win or Else: Collective Bargaining in an Age of Public Discontent* (Thousand Oaks, CA: Corwin Press, Inc., 1996), 4.

39. Myron Lieberman, *The Teacher Unions: How the NEA and AFT Sabotage Reform and Hold Students, Parents, Teachers, and Taxpayers Hostage to Bureaucracy* (New York: The Free Press, 1997), 47.

40. *Indian River County Education Association, Local 3617 v. School Board of India River County*, 4 FPER ¶ 4262 (1978), *aff'd*, 373 So. 2d 412 (Fla. 4th DCA 1979).

41. Michael Hansen. (March 17, 2009). "State Intervention an Contract Choice in the Public Teacher Labor Market." In Stephen Sawchuck (April 6, 2009). "Researchers Examine Contracts' Effects on Policy Issues." *Education Week.* Site visited May 4, 2009 at http://www.edweek.org/ew/articles/2009/04/08/28bargain _ep.h28.html, p. 2.

42. McNeil Stokes. "Labor Relations: Permissive Subject of Bargaining." Site visited 12.30.08 at http://www.acwi.org/cd/pdfs/7705_x.pdf.

43. David P. Twomey, *Labor Law and Legislation* (7th Ed.) (Cincinnati, OH: South-Western Publishing Co., 1985), 501.

44. *Ridgefield Park Education Association v. Ridgefield Park Board of Education*, 393 A.2d 278, 287 (N.J. 1978).

45. Adam Urbanski, "Improving Student Achievement Through Labor-Management Collaboration in Urban School Districts." *Educational Policy* 17 (2003): 503–518, 503–504.

46. Randall W. Eberts. Kevin Hollenbeck, and Joe A. Stone, "Teacher Unions: Outcomes and Reform Initiatives." In Ronald D. Henderson, Wayne J. Urban, and Paul Wolman (Eds.) *Teacher Unions and Education Policy: Retrenchment or Reform?* (Amsterdam: Elsevier, 2004): 51–79, 54.

47. Robert M. Carini, "Teacher Unions and Student Achievement." In Alex Molnar (Ed.) *Reform Proposals: The Research Evidence* (January 22) Education Policy Research Unit, Arizona State University (Tempe, AZ, 2002) Site visited May 12, 2002 at http://www.asu/edu/educ.epru/documents, 10.12.

48. Bruce S. Cooper and Marie-Elena Liotta, "Urban Teachers Unions Face Their Future: The Dilemmas of Organizational Maturity." *Education and Urban Society* 34 (2001) 101–118, 109.

49. Charles Taylor Kerchner, Julia E. Koppich, and Joseph G. Weeres, *Taking Charge of Quality. How Teachers and Unions Can Revitalize Schools* (San Francisco: Jossey-Bass Publishers, 1998), 14.

50. Susan Moore Johnson, "Can Schools Be Reformed at the Bargaining Table?" *Teachers College Record,* 89 (1987): 269–280, 269.

51. Susan Moore Johnson and Susan M. Kardos, "Reform Bargaining and Its Promise for School Improvement." In Tom Loveless (Ed.). *Conflicting Missions? Teachers Unions and Educational Reform* (Washington, D.C.: Brookings Institution Press, 2000), 18.

52. Kenneth E. Weick, "Educational Organizations as Loosely Coupled Systems." *Administrative Science Quarterly,* 21 (1976): 1–19.

53. Ann Bradley, "Teachers in Detroit strike over proposal for flexible schools." *Education Week* (September 9, 1992): 21.

54. Ibid.

55. Ibid.

56. Eberts et al., *supra* 46, 56.

57. Ibid.

58. Todd A. DeMitchell and Casey D. Cobb, "Teachers: Their Union and Their Profession. A Tangled Relationship." *Education Law Reporter,* 212 (2006): 1–20, 18.

59. Richard Fossey and Karen Miles, *School-Based Management in the Boston Public Schools: Why Isn't It Working?* Unpublished Report Commissioned by the Mayor of Boston (1991). A copy of this report was furnished by Richard Fossey.

60. Ibid. p. 9.

61. Todd A. DeMitchell, "Collective Bargaining, Professionalism, and Restructuring." *International Journal of Educational Reform* 2 (1993): 77–81, 79.

62. Johnson, *supra* note 23, 5.

63. See, Fossey and Miles, *supra* note 59. Collective bargaining has a strong centralizing impact on school districts. This runs counter to the reform goal of restructuring which entails a decentralization of power and authority.

Chapter 3

The Legal Framework

[T]he interest of unions, as long as you have a factory model, is seeing to
it that salaries are adequate and that they are not subject to some individual
administrator who can use them politically or in a discriminatory way.

—Al Shanker[1]

Public sector bargaining is a creature of legal mechanisms. It is through
individual state legislation built upon the foundation of federal legislation on
private sector labor relations that public sector labor relations rest. Courts[2]
and public employee labor relations board decisions give substance to the
law which guides labor relations in education and other public activities
performed by a unionized work force. Another important legal aspect of the
legal framework for public sector collective bargaining is the United States
Constitution.

The First Amendment right of association[3] allows employees to come
together to pursue common interests.[4] The landmark case supporting the right
of public employees to organize and join a union is *McLaughlin v. Tilendis*.
The First Amendment and the Fourteenth Amendment were used by the
Seventh Circuit Court of Appeals in this case involving the teachers' right
to strike wrote, "Teachers have the right of free association and unjustified
interference with teachers' associational freedom violates the due process
clause of the 14th Amendment."[5] While the Constitution allows employees
to organize it does not force employers, public or private, to bargain with the
union.[6]

Federal legislation through the 1935 National Labor Relations Act (NLRA)
established the right of employees in the private sector to organize and their
recognized right to bargain with their employer. However, it "left states free

25

to regulate labor relationships with their particular employees."[7] Most states followed the NLRA's lead several decades later granting similar rights to their public employees.

The progress of securing bargaining rights for public employees proceeded at a slow pace. This occurred in large part because of the long-standing concern about the impact of public employees organizing on the ability of government to provide essential services and the use of private sector labor tactics such as a strike against the good of the public. The watershed event, which focused public opinion, was the Boston police strike of 1919. Police officers walked off the job when the police commissioner suspended their union leaders. The walk out resulted in looting and violence. Calvin Coolidge's (a future U.S. President), the governor of Massachusetts, response to the strike captured the public's reaction: "there is no right to strike against the public safety by anybody, anywhere, anytime."[8]

This chapter will provide a legal framework for labor relations in education by first reviewing the history of teacher unions. Next, the National Labor Relations Act of 1935 will be discussed followed by its influence on the rise of public sector collective bargaining through the incorporation of its industrial union labor model. The chapter will conclude with the question of whether there is a legal retrenchment of public sector collective bargaining laws.

HISTORY OF TEACHERS UNIONS

During the early part of the 19th century, most Americans lived in dispersed farm communities or very small towns. The great majority of people lived in places with fewer than 25,000 inhabitants. The typical school was the district school, "organized and controlled by a small locality and financed by some combination of property taxes, fuel contributions, tuition payments, and state aid."[9] These one-room schools would often hold sixty to seventy students for six hours a day. The school reflected the community; it was the focus for people's lives outside of the home. The community members had little doubt that the school was theirs to control. Consequently, the degree of control that was exercised over the lives of teachers was pervasive.[10]

Teachers were dictated to in the classroom and scrutinized outside it. Because many teachers were "boarded around" at the houses of pupils' parents, the pressure on teachers to conform to the mores of the community was great. From colonial days and clearly into the common public school movement, the public has been far more restrictive in its expectations for the conduct of teachers than for the conduct of the average citizen. This unique position has ultimately been translated into a legal concept termed "exemplar."

Teachers, as exemplars, are held to a higher standard of personal conduct than the average citizen As Tyack notes: "With no bureaucracy to serve as a buffer between himself and the patrons, with little sense of being a part of a professional establishment, the teacher found himself subordinated to the community."[11] Because of their relationship to students they were and still are considered role models. Their actions away from school are judged as if their conduct would set an example for how students should act.

Teaching was without a professional anchor and the curriculum was neither articulated nor uniform. Teachers were transitory, using teaching as a way station to some other destination. With poor pay, teaching "was crowded with the very dregs, the down-and-outers of society."[12] Carl Kaestle notes that in the South and in Pennsylvania teachers were often portrayed as "drunken, foreign, and ignorant."[13] The public did not hold teachers during colonial times through the War of 1812 in high esteem. However, following the War of 1812 America saw the rise of new problems; immigration increased dramatically, urban centers grew with the attendant problems of crime and disease, and the start of the industrial revolution wrought changes in the economic and social fabric of America. In response, the "nation turned in large measure to education for the resolution of these social and economic problems."[14]

These unbureaucratized, unprofessional, inexpensive, locally dominated district schools became the target of reformers in the middle of the 19th century. This reform movement, called the common school movement, sought to bring the schools under state control, teaching a common body of knowledge in a common schoolhouse to students from different social and economic backgrounds. The drive was to professionalize the schools. In order to do this, the reformers sought to replace the village forms of governance in which laymen participated in decentralized decision making with the new bureaucratic model in which "directives flowed from the top down, reports emanated from the bottom, and each step of the educational process was carefully prescribed by professional educators."[15]

Education became bureaucratized through the rise of the common school movement. Compulsory education joined the movement after the Civil War. It not only added more students, it required more teachers to handle the increased size of the student body. This resulted, in what has become characterized by several commentators, as the feminization of teaching. School boards and superintendents needed a cheap source of labor. Men moved into the higher paying roles of school administration leaving classrooms vacant.

This void was filled by women, who were just starting to emerge from the household. The feminization of teaching, particularly elementary school teaching, came about not only because women could be hired more cheaply than men, but also because society ascribed to women a more virtuous nature than that ascribed to men. "Deportment, moral character, social obedience, domestic virtue, and firm habits were virtues to teaching, whereas over exertion in academic subjects was sometimes actually frowned upon."[16]

The large-scale entry of women into teaching had major consequences for education and the wider suffrage movement. Women played a large role in the rise of the first teachers' union and formed the backbone of the suffrage movement. Murphy underscored this development writing, "The new teachers' unions were not just women-led; they were feminist."[17] The stage was now set for the emergence of the two major teacher unions—the American Federation of Teachers (AFT) and the National Education Association (NEA).

The AFT

One of the leaders of the nascent teacher's union movement was the daughter of a stonecutter who started working at age sixteen. Later in her life she would be given the sobriquet "fiend in petticoats" by the president of Harvard College. Her teaching career began in rural schools, but the twin magnets of higher salary and further education soon drew her to Chicago, where she taught sixth grade at the South Side Hendricks School. Her name was Margaret Haley. She was the more colorful, flamboyant part of the team that took on the leadership of the Chicago Teachers Union.

The other team member, Catharine Goggin, was the strategist who alternately unleashed and reined in Margaret Haley. Goggin was one of five daughters, three of whom were schoolteachers. She was considered to be generous, often helping destitute teachers make it through difficult times. Together, Goggin and Haley were a formidable pair who worked tirelessly for the benefit of classroom teachers.

Haley and Goggin were instrumental in the early formation of the Chicago Teachers' Federation (CTF), the forerunner of the American Federation of Teachers. The CTF was organized in 1897 by some 500 teachers formerly from the National Education Association[18] with three major goals: to protect teacher pensions, to gain a pay raise (the maximum salary, which had been in effect for twenty years, was $825 a year), and to make the administration of the Chicago schools more democratic.[19]

Another rallying point was a reaction to the invasion of scientific management by administration conservatives, which engendered a feeling of powerlessness on the part of teachers.

This nascent union movement clashed with the views held by a coalition of progressive reformers, school administrators, and business leaders. These elites believed that the inherent pursuit of self-interests of a union conflicted with the selfless ideology of professionalism espoused by the reformers. For example, in 1898, the *Chicago Times-Herald* commented in an editorial that the impetus for the formation of the Chicago Teachers' Federation sprang from a "spirit not credible to the high standards of the profession."[20]

From its beginnings the CTF signaled an ideological break with the larger NEA. It was founded by elementary school classroom teachers, from which it drew its leadership, and hence it was primarily a women's union. In 1902, the CTF formed a fateful alliance that would remain one of its defining differences with the NEA to the present day—it affiliated with the Chicago Federation of Labor. This move won it the enmity of the Chicago Board of Education as well as the NEA.

The CTF's early successes involved support for a number of social welfare causes, including the successful passage of the Illinois Child Labor Law of 1903. It also successfully litigated a case against several prominent Chicago companies, such as People's Gas, Light, and Coal Company, the Chicago Telephone Company, and the Edison Electric Light Company, who had failed to pay taxes due on their capital stock and franchises. The companies were ordered to pay nearly $600,000 in back taxes.[21] The Chicago Board of Education was anything but grateful for the union's efforts to fill the board's coffers. The board voted not to expend any of those funds on teacher salaries, and it carried its disapproval of the union further by voting in 1905 to condemn the CTF's affiliation with organized labor. In spite of this, the membership of the CTF grew.

In 1915, the board upped the ante by requiring all teachers to sign a yellow dog contract—a contract requiring employees to sign an instrument agreeing as a condition of employment that they will not join a union and that they understand they will be discharged if they do so. The yellow dog contract in Chicago was called the Loeb Rule. Jack Loeb, the president of the Chicago Board of Education, told stories throughout Chicago of innocent schoolteachers who were captured by the union and forced to conform to the dominance of the women leaders of the CTF. These radical union teachers, Loeb argued, were contemptuous and rebellious toward those in authority. The attack by the board was not only against unionism but also against female trade-union leadership. In 1916, 35 teachers, most of them CTF members, were dismissed under the Loeb Rule.[22] Haley quickly reorganized her own union, breaking her powerful ties with the Chicago Federation of Labor. The CTF never regained its former strength.

This was not the only battle the CTF was waging at the time. In 1895, Nicholas Murray Butler took the helm of the NEA. He brought to the association a sense that teaching was a service akin to a religious vocation. He wedded this vision of commitment to a modern notion of professionalism that encompassed educational training and scientific inquiry. The first clash between Butler and the CTF took place at the July 1899 convention, which was held in Los Angeles.

A group of 800 teachers from Chicago boarded a train hired by the CTF bound for the summer convention in Los Angeles. The CTF had decided to launch its campaign to organize a national teachers' federation at the annual NEA meeting, because that provided the greatest concentration of teachers. The CTF did not receive a warm reception from the NEA leadership. The elements in control of the NEA labeled the Chicago teachers "revolutionists." A coalition of high school and college teachers took a critical stance toward the CTF.

The attack reached a crescendo when Butler prepared a report from the Resolutions Committee deliberations and delivered it during the last general session. Butler's report condemned the CTF for using political influence and protecting incompetents—a charge against teacher unions that would recur over the decades from various quarters. Butler called the Chicago teachers "insurrectionists" and "union labor grade teachers," whose "pernicious activities were offensive to the teaching profession."[23]

The new national teachers' organization was officially censured before it even got organized. (It is interesting to note that the strongest union members were elementary school teachers, not high school teachers. And more women were militant than men.) The Chicago Times-Herald's editorial (1898) on the formation of the Chicago Federation of Teachers charged that the CTF sprang from a "spirit not credible to the high standards of professional ethics."[24]

Rebuffed by the NEA and outmaneuvered legally by the Chicago Board of Education, the CTF lost its voice for speaking out on matters of concern to teachers. The path that the CTF was clearing was soon used by a new entity after the CTF was reorganized. In April 1916, representatives from four unions met in South Chicago to organize a national federation of teachers. This new union, the American Federation of Teachers, turned away from Margaret Haley and elected Charles Stillman of the Chicago Federation of Men Teachers as its first president. In choosing Stillman, members remarked that they needed strong leadership in times of crisis, insinuating that male leadership would provide greater strength. With this election, the union became primarily a high school teachers' union. Growth of AFT locals in the elementary schools up to World War II was minimal.

The NEA

In 1857,[25] 43 teachers from ten state teacher associations met, with the objective of upgrading teaching to a profession, elevating it above an ordinary vocation.[26] The assembled group called the new organization the National Teachers' Association. Years later, when it merged with the National Association of School Superintendents, the two organizations took the name National Education Association (NEA). At first, the teachers, even though they constituted the majority, had difficulty gaining power with in the NEA; a classroom teacher was not elected president of that body until 1928. Through 1945, only three classroom teachers had served as president.

The NEA was an association dominated by superintendents and college professors. Control of policy and control of the occupation of education rested firmly in the hands of administrators. Administration domination was evidenced in its response to a growing labor movement at the turn of the century. In a NEA meeting Margaret Haley critiqued capitalism and its impact on education. Aaron Gove, the superintendent of the Denver School District argued that teachers' involvement in the conflict between labor and capital invited the "sordidness of our personal life" where "selfishness and acquisitiveness" dominate.[27]

This signature of administration domination and reaction to unionism's perceived inherent conflict with professionalism would remain etched on the parchment of the NEA through the 1960s, as it fended off competition from the American Federation of Teachers (AFT) and came to grips with collective bargaining and its attendant union bread-and-butter issues.

From 1917 to 1920, NEA membership increased significantly. The campaign to attract new members was built around improving teacher salaries, gaining greater support for the schools, and securing greater participation of teachers in the administration of the schools. Ironically, as teacher membership increased, what power teachers did have was virtually eliminated for almost fifty years by a reorganization of the association.

Prior to NEA reorganization in 1920, the association's conventions were conducted much as New England town meetings, with each member in attendance allowed one vote. Thus, wherever the convention was held, the teachers from that city could attend en masse and out vote other delegations. This reorganization was important because the leadership of the NEA, made up primarily of administrators and college professors, wanted to move to a representative form of governance in which each state association would elect delegates to the convention, thus breaking the hold of teachers.

Prior to 1920, activists could pack the convention with local teachers. These tactics were defeated when the convention was held in Salt Lake City, Utah. "In a conservative state like Utah, teachers listened to their administrators and bowed to their authority. At the convention, teachers voted in town-meeting style to eliminate that voting format in favor of voting for delegates."[28] The NEA was dominated by administrators, with little power left over for teachers. An example of the impact of this shift is provided by Urban, who notes that of the 167 voting delegates from Illinois in the 1920s, 135 were administrators or college professors, and of the remaining 32 delegates, only 14 were elementary school teachers.[29] This increased tension between teachers and school administrators lasted until the 1970s, when the NEA transformed itself into a militant teachers' union.

Collective Bargaining in the Public Schools

The American Federation of Teachers, from its inception, was a union of teachers. "It was organized by teachers, the membership was composed of teachers, and, most important, the leadership came from classroom teachers."[30] In contrast, the NEA's early leadership came from individuals who held such positions as superintendent and college president or college professor. The AFT "differentiated itself from the NEA by defining itself as the people's union rather than as a professional association. The AFT leadership did not believe that professionalism had benefited the majority of teachers."[31] Following this theme of separate NEA and AFT visions of their organization's purposes, Theodore Martin, the NEA director of membership, proclaimed just prior to the advent of public sector collective bargaining:

> Unionism lowers the ideals of teaching, by emphasizing the selfish, though necessary economic needs of teachers—salary, hours, tenure, retirement—unionism misses altogether the finer ideals of teaching and the rich compensations that do not appear in the salary envelopes.[32]

When public sector collective bargaining started its march across the educational landscape in Wisconsin in 1959, the NEA thought it would destroy professionalism and erode the teacher's status in the community. In contrast, the AFT embraced collective bargaining arguing that teachers would gain respect because their salaries would finally be commensurate with their preparation.

In the 1960s, when public sector collective bargaining emerged in many states, the NEA's long-cherished concept of professionalism was being seriously challenged. "Teachers wanted higher salaries and better benefits, not necessarily a higher standard of respect."[33] Yet, the NEA in 1960 failed to pass a resolution, by a sound majority, that stated that collective bargaining is "compatible with the ethics and dignity of the teaching profession."[34] Soon afterwards, the NEA reversed not just its course, but its essential, long-held core philosophy.

In order to remain competitive with the AFT, the NEA changed its philosophy and tactics, which it did several years later after the success of strikes in New

York City (1962), Detroit (1964), and Philadelphia (1965), approving its first official policy supporting teachers' right to "insist" on the right to negotiate with their school board and to strike (1969).[35] The NEA came to look and act more like the AFT. Lieberman asserted that in order to "survive the challenge from the AFT, the NEA had to become a union."[36] The professional association became the union it had denigrated for decades.

Reflecting on this sea-change by the NEA in the 1960s, Bob Chase, the current president of the NEA, stated, "we took a rather quiet, genteel professional association of educators, and we reinvented it as an assertive—and, when necessary, militant—labor union."[37] Survival often dictates change, and the NEA found itself in a fight and on grounds it did not chose.

The emergence of AFT as a collective bargaining force, particularly in urban centers, in the 1960s forced the NEA to shift its focus more strongly toward teachers' self-interests.[38] The AFT and the NEA, with their different roots, came to resemble each other with the advent of public sector collective bargaining. Today, differences between the nation's two largest unions have largely, but not completely faded, and both AFT and NEA now clearly see themselves as advocates and representatives of classroom teachers and as unions. Both pursue their advocacy through politics and the policies of the collectively bargained contract.

NATIONAL LABOR RELATIONS ACT

The stock market crashed on October 24, 1929. Soon the Great Depression settled across the country bringing with it anxiety, loss of jobs and homes, and widespread, palpable fear. The economic hard times produced uncertainty resulting in a quest for security. There were more workers than jobs and workers that had jobs sought to protect them.

The New Deal legislation, the 1933 National Industrial Recovery Act (NIRA) "encouraged and emboldened workers to form unions."[39] Strikes, lock-outs, and violence marred labor relations. Employers punished, interrogated, blacklisted, and fired workers who joined unions. Workers and union leaders shut down factories and businesses. The workers intent on organizing clashed with their employers and their employer's private security forces, often backed by the police, who were equally intent on breaking the union regularly filling newspapers with stories of violence. In 1933 and 1934 the nation was rocked by large-scale work stoppages, citywide strikes, and the occupation of factories as workers sought to organize.

For example, a strike over union recognition at an auto parts plant in Toledo resulted in an extended battle between workers and the Ohio National

Guard.[40] In San Francisco the longshoremen went on strike to gain union recognition. The strike spread to include about 130,000 workers from different industries after the police and the National Guard were called in to break through the picket line.

Against this backdrop of deepening labor unrest and growing militant organizing, Senator Robert F. Wagner, a Democrat from New York, submitted a bill in 1933 entitled the National Labor Relations Act (NLRA).[41] The Secretary of Labor Frances Perkins backed the NLRA. The Act became known as the Wagner Act. On July 5, 1935 Congress enacted the NLRA; an act some considered to be the *Magna Carta* of American Labor. President Roosevelt signed the Act but he did not take part in developing it. The Act was designed to diminish labor disputes by protecting the rights of employees to organize and bargain collectively with the employer. The Act sought to safeguard "commerce from injury, impairment, or interruption, and promote the flow of commerce by removing certain recognized sources of industrial strife and unrest."[42]

The core of the Act is found in Section 7 below:

RIGHTS OF EMPLOYEES

Employees shall have the right to self-organization, to form, join, or assist labororganizations, to bargain collectively through representatives of their own choosing, and to engage in other concerted activities for the purpose of collective bargaining or other mutual aid or protection, and shall also have the right to refrain from any or all such activities except to the extent that such right may be affected by an agreement requiring membership in a labor organization as a condition of employment as authorized in section 8(a)(3) [section 158(a)(3) of this title].[43]

This section protects workers who seek to form and join unions through self-organizing efforts with the goal of selecting a representative of their choice. The employer, under the Act, must meet with the employee's exclusive representative to bargain in "good faith" the wages, benefits, and terms and conditions of employment. The Act "does not require agreement or specific outcomes."[44] The Act, in essence, altered the unilateral decision making that employers had enjoyed and replaced it with bilateral decision making on bargainable issues—wages, benefits, terms and conditions of employment.

Workers gained the full right of freedom of association and with it the protection to seek mutual aid and protection. Furthermore, the Act prohibited management from interfering with or restraining employees from exercising their right to organize and bargain or to dominate or influence a labor union. Thus, the NLRA posited a "fundamental dividing line between labor and management."[45] An *us* versus *them* mentality became codified in law. The NLRA posits in the unionized workplace, you are either labor or management—two separate and distinct categories. A dividing line between labor and management was drawn.[46] This separation becomes important once the collective bargaining rights of the NLRA are extended to public education.

The NLRA created the National Labor Relations Board, a quasi-judicial body, to administer the provisions of the Act. The Board conducts elections for exclusive representatives, determines who is in the unit—through a process of deciding which employees have a "community of interest" in their positions—and investigates charges of unfair labor practices (violations of the Act). The Board can issue "cease and desist" orders. While the Board has no enforcement mechanism, it seeks enforcement of its orders in the U.S. Courts of Appeal. Similarly, parties to the Board's decisions may seek relief through the courts as well. The Board currently consists of five members and its General Counsel is selected by the President of the United States, subject to approval by the Senate. Thirty-three regional directors assist the Board.

Prior to the passage of the NLRA only about 10 percent of the private sector workforce was organized. After the Act's passage there was a dramatic surge in union membership including both men and women. Industries such as automotive, manufacturing, steel, and rubber saw a significant increase union membership. As their membership increased so did the political clout of unions. Strikes over union recognition were reduced as the union movement's fight for recognition moved from the economic arena characterized by strikes, lockouts, and strife, to the political arena in which the rights of employees were resolved through a quasi-judicial process directed by the NLRB.

The NLRA faced a legal challenge but the Supreme Court upheld its constitutionality in *National Labor Relations Board v. Jones & Laughlin Steel Corp.* in 1937.[47] The NLRA survived the legal challenge but the Act was changed ten years later. The legislation responded to employers' and labor opponents' concern that the Act had gone too far in giving power to unions. Some asserted that the unions were corrupt and riddled with communists. Consequently, the Act needed to be rebalanced, the proponents argued.

In 1947, at the start of the Cold War, the Labor-Management Relations Act, commonly known as the Taft-Hartley Act, was passed. A Republican controlled Congress passed the Act over the veto of President Truman. Opponents of the bill dubbed it the "slave labor bill," arguing that it would usher in an era of industrial slavery. Thus, the fulcrum for balance in their estimation had been reset in the wrong direction.

The NLRA only envisioned a restraint on management's action. There were no union activities that could be considered unfair labor practices. Taft-Hartley, it was asserted, leveled the playing field by adding prohibitions on labor while retaining the prohibitions on management. It classified such union acts as secondary boycotts, sympathy strikes, which anti-union groups called "blackmail strikes," and closed shops as unfair labor practices. Another course correction of Taft-Hartley was a move to an individualistic right and a diminishment of a group right. For example, the Taft-Hartley bill outlawed closed shops and protected employees from coercive and discriminatory acts committed by the union. It also compelled union officials to take an oath that they were not communists.

The National Labor Relations Act followed by the Taft-Hartley Act pertains to the private sector. Neither extended the rights granted to private employees to government workers. "State employment was excluded because each state was viewed as a sovereign political entity not subject to Federal legislation."[48] However, starting in 1962 with President John F. Kennedy's Executive Order 10988, public sector bargaining took root. The resulting public sector collective bargaining laws were largely grafts from the NLRA and the Taft-Hartley Act. This "reliance on the NLRA as a model for state laws"[49] developed for the private sector, largely industrial union workplace has had and still has wide reaching ramifications for teachers and school districts.

INDUSTRIAL UNION LEGACY

Private sector labor law provided the foundation for public sector bargaining, which includes public school teachers.[50] "By the time teachers entered into collective bargaining in the 1960s and 1970s the word unionism largely meant industrial union."[51] This legacy from the industrial unions presents a challenge that unions and school districts face today, some 40 to 50 years later. For example, a 1997 editorial in the *Boston Globe* offered the opinion that "continuing efforts at school reform in Boston are being hampered by a factory-style approach to collective bargaining."[52] Bread-and-butter, hardball negotiations, and strikes, activities associated with the industrial union, for many, became descriptors of the emerging public sector teacher unions.

Johnson and Kardos assert that the states modeled their public sector collective bargaining laws directly on the National Labor Relations Act of 1935 discussed above.[53] The home page for the Massachusetts Labor Relations Commission underscores the historical link to the NLRA. It writes on its first page that its Commission is the "counterpart to the National Labor Relations Board.[54] "This initial choice of models to use for the public sector has had major consequences for education, given the uniqueness of public schools and a workforce that struggles with the issue of professionalism."[55] The procedures for conflict resolution, the definition of management and labor, and their respective rights were all borrowed, in many cases word for word, from the private labor sector, which embraced the industrial model.

Unions strive to protect the worker from the "whims" of management through a collectively bargained, legally enforceable contract that defines the terms and conditions of employment in addition to setting the wages and benefits associated with the job. This creates a system with two distinct parties. A "consequence of applying the factory model to education is the creation of an atmosphere of antagonism between school districts and employee unions."[56] Therefore, "industrial unionism assumes permanent adversaries. It organizes around vigorous representation of the differences between teachers and managers."[57] An *us* and *them* mentality is fostered. "Industrial-style unionism is organized around anger,"[58] which all too often colors the working relationship.[59]

Consequently, a great premium is placed on conflict management. This is so fundamental that the absence of conflict actually "arouses anxiety and uncertainty among both union leaders and school managers who fear that they will be seen as having 'gone soft.'"[60] If teachers and administrators get along too easily, is a union needed to provide protection? A relationship predicated on conflict and adversity has consequences for the long-term goals of the institution. Linda Kaboolian writes of this consequence, "adversarial relationships between teachers and school management significantly impede change efforts required to improve student achievement."[61] An outcome of collective bargaining, conflict between educators, is in opposition to the need for collaboration among educators. How to move from the "them" of bargaining to the "us" for educating students is a challenge.

When the industrial labor model is applied to education teachers become labor and administrators become management, creating a professional chasm between teachers and administrators. Lawrence Cremin points out that "even after teacher education . . . had been dramatically upgraded in the 1960s, teachers . . . still articulating the rhetoric of professionalism, and joined the union movement in large numbers and related to school administration . . . through collective bargaining rather than professional colleagueship."[62] The fact that both groups are educators with common goals and values is lost in this model. The separateness of some work activities performed by the teachers and the administrators is emphasized, and not the commonality of purpose, roots, interests, or overlapping functions. "Us" under the industrial labor is no longer inclusive, it is exclusive by defining the "them."

Consequently, the emphasis on separateness places a great premium on conflict management within the labor relations and the contract. Keane likens traditional industrial union based bargaining to a game of marbles. The Board has all the marbles and the union's job is to take them away, a zero-sum game. When I win, you lose.[63] Victory under this model is too often defined by vanquishing the other.

This focus on conflict management is further enhanced because collective bargaining is a system for creating agreement when trust is low and the union members believe that they must be protected by a legally binding instrument that spells out in some detail the terms and conditions of their work. "As a consequence, contracts must be legally explicit, anticipate contingencies, and provide for policing and enforcement. Such a system may well exaggerate the differences and diminish trust between parties."[64] The relationship becomes formal, standard, and enforced. It becomes bureaucratic with a web of rules.

Agreements that are too easily reached engender suspicion that the union has been co-opted by management, and that if the union leaders had just held out longer and fought harder the membership would have "won" more from management, or so the argument goes. If there are no battles to be won by the union, why should union members continue to shell out some of their hard-earned wages to pay union dues? If there is no conflict of interest, there is nothing to bargain and, consequently the need for a union is called into question. The ability to secure the interests of their members is what unions do and sell potential members. "[I]t is bread-and-butter issues—securing money and benefits—that have a lot to do with why unions enjoy teacher loyalty. Teachers simply believe their unions protect their interests."[65] The brand name of the union must be protected by its actions.

Workers relinquished control over the outcomes of the product of their work with the advent of industrial unionism. Decisions about what is produced and how it is produced passed from the worker into the hands of management. Workers were divorced from the formation of policy; all they can do is implement it and not develop it. For example, in several states, public employee collective bargaining law prohibits management from bargaining over matters of policy. The court in *Ridgefield Park Education Association v. Ridgefield Park Board of Education* buttressed this idea of union separation from public policy formation when it stated: "[T]he very foundation of representative democracy would be endangered if decisions of significant matters of governmental policy were left to the process of collective negotiations, where citizen participation is precluded."[66]

Furthermore, Kerchner, Koppich, and Weeres note "collective bargaining invests in the union the obligation to enhance and protect the rights of its members. It implicitly invests in management the responsibility for the health of the educational enterprise." [67] Under the industrial union model, teachers, like factory line workers, are only supposed to perform a labor function; they are not supposed to influence the outcome of the product. Uniform rules and procedures standardizing work may work well on the factory floor but not in the classroom where flexibility to changing context is a valued professional skill.

We know that this is not the reality of teaching. Classroom teachers' daily work with students is a translation and reconfiguring of policy to meet the highly individualized contexts of their classroom. Educators do not turn out mass produced students; teaching is a highly complex process calling for the use of judgment in non-routine situations. "The problem, of course, is that schools are utterly dependent on teachers *not* acting like industrial workers. Real teaching is a mixture of imperatives drawn from craft, artistic, professional, and industrial routines."[68] Classroom teachers make and adapt policy with the myriad decisions they make daily.[69] Teachers are not divorced from policy as the industrial union labor model would have us believe.

The industrial labor union model ill-serves a profession that thrives on the collegial relations of educators. La Rae Munk asserts that the factory model of labor relations "does not work well for individual professionals working in an educational setting. Teachers are not assembly line workers and their 'product' is not mass produced and interchangeable widgets, but individual educated children."[70] Like students, teachers are more than interchangeable labor parts.[71] The industrial union paradigm fits uncomfortably on the shoulders of educators. Susan Moore Johnson and Susan M. Kardos note the challenges of this paradigm for the realities of professional educators. They write,

> Industrial bargaining was good for setting rules and dividing resources, but of little use in addressing the many educational challenges that educators faced, such as reorganizing school schedules, supporting interdisciplinary teaching, effectively integrating students with special needs into regular classrooms, orengaging parents more actively in the education of their children.[72]

LEGAL RETRENCHMENT?

As noted at the beginning of this chapter, the roots of public sector collective bargaining are planted deeply in the soil of legal mechanisms. While and governors through the latter decades of the second half of the twentieth century were passing laws to create and define public sector collective bargaining, there may well be a retrenchment, a pulling back of the reach of those laws. "Overall, the 1990s redefined collective bargaining for education employees in the public sector as a fragile right that can be threatened by an unfriendly state legislature and/or governor."[73] The scrutiny of the unions has also occurred at the federal level.

For example, the U.S. Labor Department in 2003 considered rule changes, which would allow for greater detailed reporting about a union's finances. The federal rule change would only apply to the largest of teacher unions. The move was prompted by embezzlement within the Washington Teachers Union and the United Teachers of Dade (Florida).[74]

Several states in the 1990s, in many ways, reversed or stemmed the tide of legislation that strengthened public sector bargaining. Michigan has historically been a strong labor state given the dominance of the auto industry. Yet, in 1994, Governor Engler signed legislation (PA 112) that targeted teachers by changing the collective bargaining statute. The argument for the limits was to avoid work stoppages and teacher strikes. The legislation increased the number of prohibited subjects of bargaining thus preserving those topics to the sole authority of the school district. It also allowed school districts to unilaterally impose their "last best offer." One union leader called it a "stake through the heart."[75]

Oregon in 1995, made similarly major revisions to its collective bargaining laws. Among the changes were a reduction in the number of mandatory subjects of bargaining and the definitions of managerial and supervisory employees were altered. The latter resulted in the exclusion of employees who were previously covered under the law. In the same year Illinois amended the collective bargaining law limiting the scope of bargaining for K-12 and community college employees in Chicago.

Another example of retrenchment in which the rights of labor have been rolled back is found in New Hampshire. Prior to August 29, 2003, a union and a school board could negotiate into the grievance clause due process rights for a probationary teacher who was non-renewed for the following year. State law does not grant the right to a hearing for a probationary teacher whose contract is not renewed for the following year. However, the state public labor board had previously upheld contract provisions negotiated into a contract that resulted in advisory or binding arbitration for grievances filed regarding a nonrenewal. The legislature with the support of the Governor eliminated the ability to bargain such a right. The legislation also provided for a sunset for any contracts that had such a provision declaring them null and void at the expiration of the contract.[76]

The last statutory change occurred in New Mexico. In 1992, the Governor signed a public sector collective bargaining law. The bill had a sunset provision for July 1, 1999, thus forcing the legislation to be renewed. The legislature passed a successor bill but failed to muster enough votes to override the veto of the Governor—a different governor from the one who signed the original legislation. Public sector bargaining in New Mexico had a seven-year tenure before it was retired.

The genesis of public sector collective bargaining is state law. The changes in the 1990s, underscore the reality of a law-based right created within the crucible of the give and take of politics; times change and new values and interests force their way onto the public agenda. The strength of issue partisans in one decade may not be as viable in a later decade. The argument is never won forever. Critics of unions and public sector collective bargaining hail these changes with the refrain, "it is about time." Proponents of unions worry over what they perceive is an erosion of their important and hard-won rights.

For example, there were several ballot measures placed before the public in the general election of 2008. Colorado residents failed to pass Amendment 49, which would have prohibited public employee payroll deductions for union dues as well as fees for other organizations. Payroll deductions are a negotiable item, one that unions seek because it ensures a steady stream of dues without having to spend money on billing their membership and dunning delinquents. Collecting union dues is done for them by the school district and not by the union. This amendment would likely have had a negative financial impact on unions. Voters in Oregon also rejected a measure that would have impacted the unions and its members. Measure 60 was written to prohibit school districts from giving raises based on seniority and would have instituted raises based on classroom performance.[77]

Not all changes have been negative for unions. Charter schools have been touted as reform lighthouses for public education because they are unburdened from many regulations loosening the web of rules that ensnares other public schools. This release from unnecessary rules frees charter schools for innovation. A charter school appears to have questioned the argument as applied to a collectively bargained contract. Teachers at the Conservatory Lab Charter School in Brighton, Massachusetts in November of 2008 broke ranks with all charter schools in the state when they organized into a union (American Federation of Teachers Massachusetts).[78]

Do teachers who sought to work in charter schools, possibly for their distance from unionization, find that the protection of the union is desired over the conceptual argument of reform through loosening the burden of unnecessary rules? This bears watching and studying, why the change, what does unionization bring to the work of these teachers?

The legitimate needs of employees for security, reasonable wages and benefits, and working conditions that support the important work of the teacher often compete with the equally legitimate need for the efficient delivery of important public services. Unions, like most organizations which operate in the public sphere, find themselves beset from many sides, must find ways to adapt the external environment while maintaining and appropriately adjusting its internal integration to maintain its essential core function. Unions exist within a political environment developing enforceable policies through collective bargaining.

NOTES

1. Albert Shanker, "Al Shanker speaks on unions and collective bargaining," *Education Week* (May 14 1997): 35–36, 36.
2. For an example of a recent United States Supreme Court decision on public sector collective bargaining, see *Davenport v. Washington Education Association,* 127 S.Ct. 2372 (2007) in which the High Court found a Washington State statute constitutional that required public sector unions to secure affirmative authorization from its nonmembers before agency fees can be used election-related purposes. Also, for a discussion of recent court cases on labor relations in education see, Alan Miles Ruben, "The Top Ten Judicial Decisions Affecting Labor Relations in Public Education During the Decade of the 1990s: The Verdict of the Quiescent Years," *Journal of Law & Education,* 30 (2001): 247–274.
3. Freedom of Association as a Constitutional concept grew out of a series of cases in the 1950s and 1960s in which some state's sought to curb the activities of the National Association for the Advancement of Colored People. It has been asserted that the Right of Association, while not explicitly stated in the First Amendment, is derived from the rights of assembly, petition and speech. Site visited January 8, 2008 at http://supreme.lp.findlaw.com/constitution/amendment01/12.html#f194.
4. "It is beyond debate that freedom to engage in association for the advancement of beliefs and ideas is an inseparable aspect of the 'liberty' assured by the Due Process Clause of the Fourteenth Amendment, which embraces freedom of speech. . . . Of course, it is immaterial whether the beliefs sought to be advanced by association pertain to political, economic, religious or cultural matters, and state action which may have the effect of curtailing the freedom to associate is subject to the closest scrutiny." *NAACP v. Alabama ex rel. Patterson,* 357 U.S. 449 (1958): 460–461.
5. *McLaughlin v. Tilendis,* 398 F.2d 287 (7th Cir. 1968): 288.
6. Richard C. Kearney with David G. Carnevale, *Labor relations in the public sector (3rd Ed.).* (London: CRC Press, 2001): 47.
7. Robert C. Cloud, *"Davenport v. Washington Education Ass'n:* Agency Shop & First Amendment Revisited." 224 *Education Law Reporter* 617 (2007): 619.
8. Francis Russell, *A city in terror: 1919, the Boston police strike* (New York: Viking, 1975): 191.

9. Carl F. Kaestle, *Pillars of the republic: Common schools and American society, 1780–1860* (New York: Hill & Wang, 1983): 13.

10. For a discussion of how the community controlled the private lives of teachers, see Todd A. DeMitchell, "Private lives: Community control vs. professional autonomy," *Education Law Reporter* 78 (1993): 187–202.

11. David B. Tyack, *The one best system. A history of american urban education* (Cambridge, MA: Harvard University Press, 1974): 19.

12. Ruskin Teeter, *The opening up of american education: A sampler* (New York: University Press of America, 1983): 50.

13. Kaestle *supra* note 9, 20.

14. Todd A. DeMitchell, "Educating America: The nineteenth-century common school promise in the twentieth century, a personal essay." *International Journal of Educational Reform* 9 (2000): 80.

15. Teeter, supra note 12, 40.

16. Marjorie Murphy, *Blackboard unions: The AFT and NEA, 1900–1980* (Ithaca, NY: Cornell University Press, 1990): 12.

17. Tyack *supra* note 11, 61.

18. Charles J. Coleman, *Managing labor relations in the public sector* (San Francisco: Jossey-Bass Publishers, 1990): 40.

19. Murphy, *supra* note 16, 62.

20. Charles T. Kerchner and Douglas E. Mitchell, *The changing idea of a teachers' union* (Philadelphia: Falmer Press, 1988): 56.

21. Anthony M. Cresswell and Michael J. Murphy, with Charles T. Kerchner, *Teachers, unions, and collective bargaining in public education* (Berkeley, CA: McCutchan Publishing Company, 1980): 71.

22. Murphy, *supra* note 16, 83.

23. Ibid. 54.

24. Kerchner and Mitchell *supra* note 20, 56.

25. The earliest educational association was the American Institute of Instruction. Charles J. Coleman, *Managing labor relations in the public sector* (San Francisco: Jossey-Bass Publishers, 1990): 35.

26. Cresswell and Murphy, *supra* note 21, 59.

27. Murphy, *supra* note 16, 59.

28. Joel Spring, *The American school 1642–1990* (2nd ed.) (New York: Longman, 1990): 272.

29. Wayne Urban, *Why teachers organize* (Detroit: Wayne State University Press, 1982): 127.

30. William A. Streshly and Todd A. DeMitchell, *Teacher unions and TQE: Building quality labor relations* (Thousand Oaks, CA: Corwin Press, Inc, 1994): 9.

31. Dan Goldhaber, "Are teacher unions good for students? In Jane Hannaway and Andrew J. Rotherham (Eds). *Collective bargaining in education* (Cambridge, MA: Harvard Education Press, 2006): 143.

32. Kerchner and Mitchell, *supra* note 20, 57.

33. Streshly and DeMitchell, *supra* note 30, 10.

34. L. Dean Webb and M. Scott Norton, *Human resources administration: Personnel issues and needs in education* (5th Ed.) (Upper Saddle River, NJ: Merrill Prentice Hall, 2009): 261.

35. Ibid. 263.

36. Myron Lieberman, *The teacher unions: How the nea and aft sabotage reform and hold students, parents, teachers, and taxpayers hostage to bureaucracy* (New York: The Free Press, 1997): 26.

37. Bob Chase, "The new NEA: Reinventing teacher unions for a new era." Remarks Before the National Press Club. Washington, D.C. (February 7, 1997). Site accessed January 6, 1998 at www.nea.org, p. 2.

38. Terry M. Moe, "A union by any other name," *Education Next* (2001). Site visited December 4, 2004 at http://www.educationnext.org/20013/3/38moe.htm.

39. John W. Budd, *Labor relations: Striking a balance* (Boston: McGraw-Hill, 2005): 123.

40. See, Philip A. Korth and Margaret R. Beegle, *I remember it like today: The auto-lite strike of 1934* (East Lansing, MI: Michigan State University Press (1988).

41. 29 U.S.C. §§ 151–169.

42. Section 1 [§ 151].

43. Section 7. [§ 157].

44. Budd, *supra* note 39, 157.

45. Charles Taylor Kerchner and Julia Koppich, "Organizing around quality: The struggle to organize mind workers," in Ronald D. Henderson, Wayne J. Urban, and Paul Wolman (Eds.) *Teacher unions and education policy: retrenchment or reform?* (Amsterdam: Elsevier, 2004): 205.

46. Ibid.

47. *National Labor Relations Board v. Jones & Laughlin Steel Corp*, 301 U.S. 1 (1937). The United States Supreme Court held that the Act was based on the Commerce Clause because labor-management disputes were directly related to interstate commerce. Unregulated industrial activities, the High Court reasoned, had the potential to disrupt and restrict interstate commerce.

48. Carol Wright and David E. Gundersen, "Unions and teachers: Differences in the state of the nation." *ASLB Journal of Employment and Labor Law* 2 (2004): 2.

49. Susan Moore Johnson, "Paralysis or possibility: What do teacher unions and collective bargaining bring?" in Ronald D. Henderson, Wayne J. Urban, and Paul Wolman (Eds.) *Teacher unions and education policy: Retrenchment or reform?* (Amsterdam: Elsevier, 2004): 47.

50. The exception to the NLRA as the touchstone for public sector bargaining is the Lloyd-LaFollette Act guaranteeing federal workers the right to organize—postal workers in 1863 formed the first federal employee organization—and to petition Congress regarding grievances. William L. Sharp *Winning at collective bargaining: Strategies everyone can live with* (Lanham, MD: The Scarecrow Press, Inc., 2003): 1–2.

51. Charles Taylor Kerchner and Julia E. Koppich, "Organizing around quality: examples and policy options from the frontiers of teacher unionism." Site Visited February 9, 2003 at http://63.197.216/crcl/mindworkers/udpages/fulldoc.htm.

52. Author, "Time for teaching" in *The Boston Globe* (September 8, 1997), A14.

53. Susan Moore Johnson and Susan M. Kardos, "Reform Bargaining and Its Promise for School Improvement," in Tom Loveless (Ed.), *Conflicting missions? Teachers unions and educational reform* (Washington, DC: Brookings Institution Press, 2000): 8.

54. http://www.mass.gov/lrc/. Site visited January 26, 2008.

55. Todd A. DeMitchell, "A reinvented union: A concern for teaching, not just teachers," *Journal of Personnel Evaluation in Education*, 11 (1998): 257.

56. La Rae G. Munk, *Collective bargaining: Bringing education to the table* (Midland, MI: Mackinac Center for Public Policy, 1998): 16.

57. Charles Taylor Kerchner and Krista D. Caufman, "Building the Airplane While It's Rolling Down the Runway," in Charles Taylor Kerchner and Julia E. Koppich, *A union of professionals: Labor relations and educational reform* (New York: Teachers College Press, 1993): 15.

58. Julie E. Koppich, "Getting started: A primer on professional unionism," in Charles T. Kerchner and Julie E. Koppich, *A Union of Professionals: Labor Relations and Educational Reform* (New York: Teachers College Press, 1993): 200.

59. In a study of teacher's perceptions of the compatibility of being a union member and a professional, 64 percent of the responding teachers agreed or strongly agreed, with 22 percent disagreeing or strongly disagreeing that their professional activities are enhanced through collegial relationships with administrators. By almost three-to-one the teachers believe that collegial relations with administrators is important. However, on another question 47 percent agreed or strongly agreed that the contract separates educators into us (teachers) and them (administrators). Thirty percent agreed or strongly disagreed with the proposition. Todd A. DeMitchell and Casey D. Cobb, "Teachers: Their Union and Their Profession. A Tangled Relationship," *Education Law Reporter*, 212 (2006): 15. Teachers need to work with administrators but they become adversaries through collective bargaining.

60. Kerchner and Mitchell, *supra* note 20, 237.

61. Linda Kaboolian, *Win-Win labor management collaboration in education: Breakthrough practices to benefit students, teachers, and administrators* (Mt. Morris, IL: Education Week Press, 2005): 24.

62. Lawrence A, Cremin, *American education: The Metropolitan experience 1876–1980* (New York: Harper & Row Publishers, 1998): 500. The original quote included nursing education, nurses, and hospital administrators parallel to teachers and school administrators.

63. William G. Keane, *Win win or else: Collective Bargaining in an age of public discontent* (Thousand Oaks, CA: Corwin Press, Inc., 1996). Keane states that the focus of our concern must move from "How much can we get (union) or keep (management/Board)?' to 'How can we fairly (to students, staff, and community) and wisely use the resources available to us?' (11).

64. Cresswell and Murphy, *supra* note 21, 479.

65. Steve Farkas, Jean Johnson, and Ann Duffett, *Stand by me: What teachers really think about unions, merit pay and other professional matters* (Washington, DC: Public Agenda, 2003): 17.

66. *Ridgefield Park Education Association v. Ridgefield Park Board of Education*, 393 A.2d 278 (N.J. 1978), 287.

67. Charles Taylor Kerchner, Julia E. Koppich, and Joseph G. Weeres, *United mind wokers: Unions and teaching in the knowledge society* (San Francisco: Jossey-Bass Publishers, 1997): 137.

68. Charles Taylor Kerchner and Julia E. Koppich, "Organizing around quality" in Tom Loveless (Ed.), Conflicting missions? Teachers unions and educational reform (Washington, DC: Brookings Institution Press, 2000): 284 (emp. in original).

69. See Michael J. Lipsky, *Street-level bureaucrats: Dilemmas of the individual in public services* (New York: Russell Sage Foundation Publications, 1983) for a discussion of how teachers and other street-level bureaucrats while not making policy for an organization adapt and implement policies within the confines of the classroom to better render their service to the public.

70. La Rae G. Munk, *Collective bargaining: Bringing education to the table* (Midland, MI: Mackinac Center for Public Policy, 1998): 16.

71. Johnson and Kardos, *supra* note 53, 10, state that industrial unionism assumes that "similarly skilled workers are interchangeable and should be treated alike."

72. Ibid. 19.

73. David J. Strom and Stephanie S. Baxter, "From the statehouse to the schoolhouse: How legislatures and courts shaped labor relations for public education employees during the last decade," *Journal of Law & Education* 30 (2001): 296.

74. Julie Blair, "Labor Dept. Proposes to Heighten Scrutiny of Teachers' Unions." *Education Week* (July 9, 2003): 26.

75. William Lowe Boyd, David N. Plank, and Gary Sykes, "Teacher Unions in Hard Times," in Tom Loveless (Ed.) *Conflicting missions? Teacher unions and educational reform* (Washington, DC: Brookings Institution Press, 2001): 180.

76. New Hampshire RSA 273-A:4.

77. *Education Week*, "State Ballot Measures" (November 12, 2008), 18–19.

78. James Vaznis, Teachers unionize at charter school, a first for Mass. *The Boston Globe* (November 26, 2008) 1, 10.

Section II

Politics

Chapter 4

Conflict and Community

> At their worst, unions and school districts are two prisoners manacled to-
> gether and slugging it out with their free hands. At their most productive,
> they are self-interested partners in a joint civic venture.[1]

Senator Hillary Rodham Clinton, in a television advertisement for her candidacy for the Democratic nominee for President of the United States, advised, "Know when to stand your ground and when to find common ground."[2] She was talking about politics, but she could easily have been discussing collective bargaining.

Collective bargaining and unionization imply that there is a conflict of interest and a community of interest between the two parties, the union and management. There is a conflict of interest in that employees through their union pursue their self-interests. Those self-interests include secur-ing the best wage and benefits as well as the best working conditions for the employee and for the employer receiving the optimal work from the employee to meet goals of providing an effective and efficient educational program. There is a community of interest as well. Both labor and man-agement want to establish a good work place that allows the employee to maximize his/her work.

Teachers' interests may include a high wage, broad benefits, low class size, control over their instruction, influence over the curriculum, and maximizing their options. Management's interests may include providing a reasonable competitive wage, cost controlled benefits, curriculum alignment through grade levels and subjects and across schools, accountability for student out-comes and providing a cost-effective instructional program. These separate interests are legitimate and many times in conflict with each other.

Collective bargaining embraces both conflict and community. If there is only conflict there may be no way to achieve a contract. If there is only a community of interest, is there anything to bargain? Agreement is assured. Both are part of the bargaining process and both are legitimate. If there is no community of interest that can be served through bargaining there will be nothing but conflict. The tension between conflict and community is inherent and normal. Both are legitimate. How to find the community of interest and to capitalize on it while simultaneously realizing that conflict is real and will not go away is the challenge of labor relations both at the negotiating table and away from the table.

This chapter will start with the conflict found in labor relations by reviewing the three major vehicles for addressing conflict, grievances, impasse, and unfair labor practices. This section starts with the twin propositions that grievances are our friends and school administrators should wear their grievance hat when processing grievances. Most of my students are very skeptical about both of these propositions until we talked about what they mean. Hopefully, I have won some converts. The second section will review bargaining concepts that I use in my classes and that form the core of my approach to labor relations, including bargaining.

Conflict is not confined to collective bargaining. It is, in many ways, a constant in social life. School administrators encounter conflict in many different settings apart from the contract. Building conflict resolution skills is a vital skill for leaders whether they are formal or informal leaders. However, this section is not an exhaustive discussion of the topic of conflict resolution.[3]

CONFLICT OF INTERESTS: LABOR DISPUTES

Clark Kerr considered labor relations to be a form of conflict driven in large part by differences in needs and desires. He characterized this conflict as normal if not necessary. He wrote, "If labor and management are to retain their institutional identities, they must disagree and must act on this disagreement. Conflict is essential to survival."[4] Conflict leads to disputes and because public sector collective bargaining was instituted to achieve labor peace and harmony in the workplace,[5] consequently, mechanisms were developed to address conflict. Conflict resolution is used when managing the contract (grievances), bargaining the contract (impasse), and labor relations (unfair labor practices).

Grievances: Our Friend and the Grievance Hat

It is important to start with what is a grievance. A grievance is an alleged violation, misapplication, or misinterpretation of a specific section of the collective bargaining agreement. It is not a disagreement with any decision that a school administrator makes. All conflicts are not grievances. Grievances that access the grievance procedures of the contract must be contained to addressing problems arising from the application and/or interpretation of the contract. To use the grievance procedure for any and all disagreements is to expand the contract without the benefit of bargaining. The grievance process was fashioned through the collective bargaining process to address problems associated with conflict regarding the contract.

There is a tendency to believe that grievances are bad things and that they are indicative of administrative failure or employee venality and retaliation. I prefer to approach grievances differently. Grievances can be our friends. They provide a process for defining what the contract means. Sometimes it is a difficult process and one that can be overused and abused, but it is a legitimate conflict resolution procedure. All too often administrators react negatively to grievances with displays of anger, embarrassment, and hurt feelings. While these emotions are real, they have no place within the administration of the contract. I have had my fair share of grievances filed while I was a principal. I adopted the following and found it effective.

- Keep the process professional, and keep the responses focused on the alleged violations of the contract. An emotional response to grievances enables the process to be used as a cudgel to keep administrators off balance and under control. Having a grievance filed is neither a badge of distinction nor a badge of shame.
- Understand the grievance using good listening skills. If the grievance is not clear or if it is vague seek clarity by asking questions. You cannot resolve that which you do not understand.
- Know specifically what section(s) of the contract are alleged to have been violated, misinterpreted, or misapplied. Do not accept general statements. This keeps a focus so only the problem stated in the grievance is solved. Do not allow the filing of a grievance to turn into a fishing expedition for any disagreement.
- If the grievance does not cite a specific section of the contract, reject the grievance because it is not a grievance. It may be a problem, but it is not a grievance. It may be a problem, but it is not a problem with the contract.
- What is the proposed remedy advanced in the grievance? Is it reasonable? Does it solve the grievance or does it create unintended consequences? Always ask what does this mean in the future if I implement this remedy.

- Consult with other administrators, particularly at the District Office as to whether there have been similar grievances filed on this section. Consult the grievance log.
- Both the union and management can use grievances to work through differences of opinion and help to resolve conflict or it can be used to heighten and sustain conflict. Management cannot control the union's use of the process; it can control its response to the use of the process. This approach does not mean that management can't respond firmly and clearly when the process is being abused. It does mean that grievances are not the enemy of good leadership. They can help to explore how the contract is implemented and whether it applies to new and novel situations.
- Grievances should trigger an analysis of the targeted contract section for ambiguity, relevance, and efficiency.
- Good leadership on both sides takes these opportunities to respond to conflict to model professional, honest behavior, to improve relationships, and to move the institution forward. This furthers a community of interest out of a conflict of interest.

Using the description of the small grievance hat provides a vision that grievances are a specific conflict resolution tool. Grievances are not the only strategy; they are, however, the one that both parties agreed to use in the specific case of conflict involving the contract. It is unwise to use the grievance process to solve conflict that arises outside of the contract. Develop strategies for solving those other conflicts. Only the contract can fit under the small grievance hat.

Grievances can be our friend when we approach them as opportunities to resolve conflicts and occasions to gain a greater understanding of the contours and conditions of work under a contract. Grievances can remain our friend when they are confined to the job they were created to do and apply the contract consistently and fairly. Grievances become unwieldy when they are used to solve all problems and misunderstandings. The grievance process was bargained in good faith, it must be applied in good faith.

Many, if not most, contracts have arbitration as part of the grievance process. Arbitration related to the enforcement of a contract is called rights arbitration. When arbitration is used to settle a contract it is called interest arbitration. The use of interest arbitration is limited most often to public safety.

Arbitration of a grievance is either advisory or binding. This is a bargainable subject. Advisory arbitration results in a written position delivered by the arbitrator. It as its name implies it is an advisory opinion; it cannot be imposed on the parties. However, binding arbitration is a quasi-judicial opinion; it must be implemented. It is less of a problem solving character and more of a judicial character. An arbitrator's task is to interpret the contract and apply it to the dispute/grievance. Most collective bargaining contracts include language that states that the arbitrator shall have no power to alter, add to, or subtract from the specific language of the contract.[6] In an interesting case out of Indiana, an arbitrator's award was upheld by the state Court of Appeals. The arbitrator ordered the school district to issue a letter of apology for disciplining a teacher in violation of the collective bargaining agreement.[7]

The arbitration hearing is more of a courtroom hearing in which the advocates for both parties extensively prepare, evidence is presented and witnesses are questioned. Arbitrators use three elements: the language of the contract, the intent of the parties (see the discussion on managing information in chapter 7), and past practice[8] to reach a decision.

School districts that argue against binding arbitration assert that the school board is the elected body and that it should not give up its decision making authority to an outside party. While the argument makes a good political statement it may not have the force of law. Many state public employment boards, similar to the National Labor Relations Board,[9] have held that a workable grievance procedure must end with some form of binding arbitration from an outside party. If the contract does not have a "workable" grievance procedure, the grievance may be elevated to an unfair labor practice. Thus, a third party makes a binding decision anyway, destroying the argument for not negotiating binding arbitration.

An advantage in bargaining binding arbitration is that it provides an opportunity to clearly state if there are sections of the contract that are not appropriate to take to arbitration. This is called positive assurance. All sections of a contract are considered open to the grievance process including arbitration if it is contained in the contract. If a section of the contract, such as the content of an evaluation or observation, is considered inappropriate for third party arbitration, that section can be bracketed with a statement that it is not subject to either the grievance process or to arbitration. Positive assurance is then gained because both parties have agreed to clear, unambiguous language through a meeting of the minds at the bargaining table.

All conflicts are not grievances. Grievances that access the grievance procedures of the contract must be contained to addressing problems arising from the application or interpretation of the contract. To use the grievance procedure for any and all disagreements is to expand the contract without benefit of bargaining. This does not mean that the school administrator should disregard a concern about a decision that it is not a grievance, it just means that a separate conflict resolution process must be used. Employees have a right to access appropriate processes to address legitimate concerns. To do less by management is to injure labor relations.

Impasse

Impasse is another conflict resolution process. It is used when negotiations on the contract have stalled to the point that no further progress is being made and is not likely to be made. Impasse should only be declared when no movement is being made on any of the sections of the contract. As long as a single issue is being negotiated with some success—ongoing discussion and/or trading proposals—impasse should not be declared. The process for declaring impasse and instituting the impasse procedures vary by states.

Impasse typically involves two actions: mediation followed by fact-finding. Mediation involves a third-party mediator meeting with the two parties separately and at times together. The goal of the mediator is to get an agreement. The goal is not to fashion a wise agreement; it is to get agreement. One state mediator working with a school district and a union representing teacher aides summed it up this way, "Tell me what it will take to wrap it up."[10] Deborah Kolb, in her research on mediators characterized state mediators as the ones who mediate public sector collective bargaining as deal makers. For example in her analysis she quotes a mediator, "I come in, I want to make a deal. I need something to work with."[11]

If mediation is not successful, the parties go to fact-finding. Fact-finding is advisory. The goal is for each party to present their best argument for their position using facts to support their position. The fact-finder analyzes the position of both parties and renders a decision as to which positions are supported by the facts. This decision is typically advisory which reduces the effectiveness and efficiency of fact-finding as a conflict resolution strategy.

Unfair Labor Dispute

The last labor dispute mechanism is an unfair labor practice. Whereas, a grievance is an allegation of a violation of the contract, an unfair labor practice is an allegation of a violation of the state public sector collective bargaining law. Unfair labor practices are state specific with each state defining what constitutes an unfair labor practice. A violation of good faith bargaining by making a unilateral change in wages, benefits, or terms and conditions of employment is a common unfair labor practice. Another is interfering with the union's right exclusive representation through management either offering inducements or threats.

Unfair labor practices can be filed by the union against management/employer, or by the employer against the union. The latter are the most common petitioner with less unfair labor practices being filed by management. A third option is for an employee to file a grievance against the union. When this happens it is typically an allegation of the failure of the duty of fair representation. For example, in New York a teacher filed an unfair labor practice, in part, against his union alleging a violation of the duty of fair representation when the union decided not to pursue one of his grievances.[12] Unions are not required to pursue all grievances to arbitration.

BUILDING A COMMUNITY OF INTEREST

As stated above bargaining has a tension between conflict of interests and a community of interests. The conflict will not go away. There is, however, an inherent community of interest founded on the professional service rendered by educators through the organization of a school. A challenge is how to maintain and expand that community of interest within the confines of the conflict of interests There is no silver bullet, no magic incantation that makes bargaining easy, turning it into a "Kumbaya moment." It is hard work, but anchoring bargaining and labor relations with concepts and approaches helps.

We are all negotiators, whether we sit at a formal table of two sides, we negotiate many things in our life. It is one of the basic ways by which one individual gets something from another. An Italian diplomat, Daniel Vare, once said that negotiation is the "art of letting them have your way."[13] "It is a back-and-forth communication designed to reach agreement when you and the other side have some interests that are shared and others that are opposed."[14] Negotiations are predicated on getting the other side to say yes to what you want. Individuals negotiate because they believe that they can get something that they could not without negotiations.

The following will discuss two well-known and respected books that set the stage for negotiating at the table or away from the table.

Getting to Yes

Roger Fisher and William Ury as part of the Harvard Negotiations Project developed the concept of "principled negotiations." The four basic points of principled negotiations are:

1. People: separate the people from the problem,
2. Interests: focus on interests, not positions,
3. Options: Generate a variety of possibilities before deciding what to do, and
4. Criteria: Insist that the result be based on some objective standard.[15]

These four aspects of principled negotiations can produce a wise agreement through fair negotiations. A wise agreement should be efficient, and should improve or at least not damage the relationship between parties. As stated in the introduction, it is the relationship between the parties that will carry on long after the ink from the signatures has dried. The relationship will be the indicator of the success of negotiations. Signing a contract is not the measure of success of negotiations; success is measured by how the parties treat each other afterwards, has their relationship improved and can the new contract be implemented and managed by fairness and trust or will suspicion and the need to get even define the relationship? Embattled and embittered teachers and administrators signal a continuation of hostilities following the brief lull of the signing. Battle lines for the next round of negotiations get drawn early.

Fisher and Ury's first rule of negotiating is "Don't bargain over positions." There is comfort in having and holding a position. The anchor of a position, however, tends to keep you in one place when options and possibilities best serve the interests you are pursuing at the table. Protecting positions often produces unwise and inefficient agreements. Bargaining over positions often results in the negotiator identifying worth as a negotiator with holding and securing the position—losing the position equals losing face at the table and with the constituency. Too often "[p]ositional bargaining becomes a contest of wills"[16] with the requisite winner and loser.

Instead of adopting a position and bargaining to secure that position, Fisher and Ury suggest that you focus on your interests and not on your position. The following are some of the suggestions to advance your interests at the table:

- Talk about your interests. One of the purposes of negotiating is to serve your interests.
- Be hard on the problem but soft on the people. You are trying to resolve the problem not harm individuals or the relationship. "If negotiators view themselves as adversaries in a personal face-to-face confrontation, it is difficult to separate their relationship form the substantive problem."[17]
- Put the problem before your answer. Give your interests and reasoning first and your conclusions or proposals later.
- "You will satisfy your interests better if you talk about where you would like to go rather than about where you have come from."[18]

If the other side wants to engage in positional bargaining, they suggest trying the following:

- When the other side sets forth their position, neither reject it nor accept it. Look for their interest that lies behind it. What are they seeking from this language? Treat their proposal as one possible solution. This is consistent with good faith bargaining.

- Instead of asking the other side to accept or reject your ideas, ask them what is wrong with the idea.
- Ask questions and then remember to pause, giving them time to generate answers. Silence is too little used; often silence makes individuals uncomfortable and they seek to fill the silence. Also, it is important to remember that when your mouth is closed as you listen, it is hard to fit your foot into it.[19]
- Question their tactics, not their personal integrity.
- Don't undermine your credibility by making extreme demands that both parties know will be abandoned. In other words, don't squander credibility, it is hard to get and even harder to maintain.
- Yield to reason, not pressure.

Just being nice (Can't we just get along?), however, is not the answer. A hard game dominates a soft game. This does not mean that you should yield to pressure or let yourself be coerced; yield only to principle and reason not pressure. The outcome of principled negotiations should improve relations but focusing on the relationship to the exclusion of furthering your interests runs the risk of attaining neither. The hard game should focus on the problem and not the people. A wise agreement is not reached by giving in; too often it feeds the appetite from the other side to gain more by pressuring more. Don't allow it to become effective.

A strategy that Fisher and Ury suggest is developing a Best Alternative to a Negotiated Agreement (BATNA). They assert that it "will protect you against both accepting an agreement you should reject and rejecting an agreement you should accept."[20] A BATNA provides a standard by which negotiations can be measured in satisfying management or the union's interests. Maurer asserts that a BATNA removes mental pressure to reach an agreement and it gives a criterion for measuring proposals.[21] Fisher and Ury believe that in most circumstances the greater danger is being too committed to reaching an agreement and being unduly pessimistic about negotiations being broken off. A well-developed BATNA increases the ability to improve the terms of any negotiated agreement.

Getting Together

The sequel to *Getting to Yes* is *Getting Together*.[22] This book takes the basic ideas about negotiation (stated above) and focuses on the relationship of shared and conflicting interests. It is notable that Fisher branches out from the first book by choosing to explore in greater detail the relationship that exists between the parties. The overall theme of the book is the importance of pursuing a "working relationship," one that can deal with the inherent differences of a relationship.

In many ways, *Getting Together* may be the beginning point. Collective bargaining in education involves negotiations between two parties who know each other. They come to the table with a relationship and will have a relationship once they leave the table. If the relationship is poor before bargaining begins, there is diminished hope that acrimony will dry up and wither away on its own. In contrast, a strong relationship smoothes the path for mutual gain. An improved labor relationship is one of the themes of this book.

Getting to Yes developed principled negotiations, *Getting Together* advances an Unconditionally Constructive Strategy. This strategy is designed to improve relationships without harming substantive interests pursued at the bargaining table. Their guidelines are not directed on how to be good, but rather on how to be effective. "They derive from a selfish hard-headed concern with what each of us can do, in practical terms, to make a relationship work better."[23] In a nutshell, an unconditionally constructive strategy states, "Do only those things that are good for the relationship and good for us, whether or not they are reciprocated."[24]

The unconditionally constructive strategy seeks a good substantive outcome for both parties, inner peace ("We want to be able to say: 'I can work things out with these people.'"[25]), and an ability to deal with differences. As discussed above collective bargaining takes place in environment with a community of interests and a conflict of interests. Differences and conflict in relationships is normal; their appearance does not signify that the relationship is in crisis.

The major themes of their strategy are summarized below:

1. Balance reason and emotion: We often act emotionally rather than logically. Emotions are a necessary part of us; we do not choose our emotions, they just happen. Too much emotion can cloud judgment and overwhelm reason and too little can impair motivation and judgment. Parties at the bargaining table should neither press their emotions nor ignore them. They write, "I should no more ignore them than I should ignore any other important fact in negotiation. But my emotional state may cause me to make poor judgments about what to say and what to do."[26]
2. Understanding: See how they see things. Whether or not the parties agree is not the major point; rather trying to understand each other's perceptions, values, and interests is the major point. One party does not have to accept the other's perception, values, and interests but understanding them allows for a greater chance of finding a community of interest for them.

3. Good communication: Always consult before deciding (ACBD). Fisher and Brown identify three barriers to effective communication; we assume that there is no need to talk; we communicate in one direction by telling; and we send mixed messages.[27] Good communication facilitates any relationship; poor communication harms relationships. Developing a habit of communicating is important. Adopting a strategy of no surprises can be helpful. No surprises means, I communicate early so as to not surprise the other party, possibly forcing them into defensiveness and a feeling of being disregarded. It also means that I don't like surprises either.

4. Reliability: Both parties work on being trustworthy. Communication is a wasted opportunity if it is not believed. Fisher and Brown pose the following questions: Is our conduct erratic? Do we communicate carelessly? Do we treat even clear promises lightly? And, Are we deceptive or dishonest?"[28] Be wholly trustworthy but not wholly trusting.

5. Persuasion, not coercion is most helpful: As stated in *Getting To Yes,* one should not give into coercion. The less likely, according to the authors, that the outcome will reflect the concerns of both parties the less likely it will be accepted. Coercion tends to damage the quality of an agreement: a coerced agreement may not have been crafted to meet the interests of both parties; it may not benefit from creative thinking, and its legitimacy as measured by standards of fairness are questioned. Individuals do not like to feel that they are being coerced. If it doesn't work against me, why would it work for me?

6. Mutual acceptance: Acknowledges the long-term relationship. Acceptance does not mean approval; it means accepting the other parties right to have views that differ. Good relations are not easy to achieve; they involve hard work. However, giving in to appease does not work. "It may avoid arguments, but it also eliminates the opportunity to learn how to talk through problems and to become skillful at reaching solutions."[29]

If labor and management treat each other with respect and pay attention to the process of collective bargaining, then it will be easier for both parties to have a sustained and shared win at the table and in the schools. *Getting To Yes* and *Getting To Together* may help to build on the community of interest that exists in our schools, while not negating the conflict of interest that exists. Fisher and Brown conclude:

> Discussing honestly our joint ability to deal with differences is almost certain to reduce misunderstandings, improve communication, and convey the message that each of accepts the other as someone with a contribution to make in dealing with joint problems. A good working relationship will work even better when we work on it together.[30]

How we respond to the other side is within our control. We can't control the other, we can control ourselves and how we respond. Do we seek to expand the community of interest or contract it? Do we seek to emphasize differences and embrace our conflicts? Each party decides how to answer these questions. "[I]t would be a mistake to define a good relationship as one in which we agree easily, just as it would be a mistake to define a good road as one that is easy to build."[31]

A last consideration of a community of interest is win–win bargaining which seeks to emphasis the community of interest. This begs the question of whether there has to be losers when bargaining. While there are many forms of win–win bargaining, this brief discussion will look at one representative author, William Keane, as an example. Keane writes, "The basic premise of bargaining in a win–win mode is the assumption that both parties see the best interests of their constituents are most efficiently served by helping the other party meet the interests of its own constituents simultaneously."[32] He offers five principles for those who pursue win–win bargaining.

1. Facilitate the Growth of Trust; Don't Demand It
2. Separate Resource-Allocation Issues From Problem-Resolution Issues
3. Start by Exchanging Problems, Not Solutions
   Presentation of problems:
   A. This is our problem.
   B. These are the reasons that this issue is a problem for us.
   C. Here are the facts that demonstrate that this is a problem.[33]
4. Brainstorm Solutions for Problems
5. Freely Share Relevant Information

Some common points of win–win bargaining include, frequent year-round meetings to discuss problems as they come up rather than waiting for the contract to expire, keeping communications open, helping each other win, using a problem solving approach rather than trying to win points, and developing a trusting relationship. Some have recommended that outside negotiators not be used arguing that the people at the table must have stake in the outcome and in the relationship. Trust and reliability are critical traits.

There does not appear to be any magic about win–win bargaining. The approach to win–win makes sense whether it is called win–win or just plain old-fashioned bargaining that wants to get the job done. What may set it apart is the conscious decision that both parties want to do something different and commit to making a difference at the bargaining table and away from the bargaining table. It acknowledges the conflict of interest and focuses on building and emphasizing the community of interest.

At the end of the day of bargaining, there is no magic formula or perfect process that moves everyone to win–win bargain resulting in the "Elegant Solution." It is hard work that does not end. The garden must always be tended to lest it be overgrown with weeds and revert back to its original wild state. If there is any magic in the process it is in the individuals who remain committed to doing it differently and trying to do it better. Individuals who are committed to improving the relationship make the difference.

NOTES

1. Charles Taylor Kerchner and Krista D. Caufman, "Building the airplane while it's rolling down the runway," in Charles Taylor Kerchner and Julia E. Koppich, *A union of professionals: Labor relations and educational reform* (New York: Teachers College Press, 1993): 2.

2. Senator Hillary Rodham Clinton. (December 17, 2007). WMUR Channel 9 (ABC affiliate).

3. For an expanded discussion of conflict resolution within a bargaining environment, I suggest the following:
   - Max Bazermann and Margaret Neale, *Negotiating rationally* (Cambridge, MA: Harvard University Press, 2006).
   - Robert H. Mnookin, Scott R. Peppet, and Andrew S. Tulumello, *Beyond winning: Negotiating to create value in deals and disputes* (Cambridge, MA: The Belknap Press of Harvard University, 2004).
   - Douglas Stone, Bruce Patton, and Sheila Heen, *Difficult conversations: How to discuss what matters* (New York: Viking, 1999).

4. Clark Kerr, "The Nature of Industrial Conflict," in E. Wight Bakke, Clark Kerr, and Charles W. Anrod (Eds.), *Unions, management, and the public* (San Diego, CA: Harcourt Brace Jovanovich, 1967): 246.

5. In New Hampshire, public sector collective bargaining was developed to "foster harmonious and cooperative relations between public employers and their employees to protect the public by encouraging the orderly and uninterrupted operation of government." Chapter 490, December 21, 1975. Statement of Policy New Hampshire Revised Statutes Annotated 273-A. Site visited January 17, 2009 at http://www.nh.gov/pelrb/. In Illinois, "the Illinois General Assembly declared the purpose of the IELRA was to promote orderly and constructive relationships between educational employees and their employers, recognizing that harmonious relationships are required between educational employees and their employers." Site visited January 17, 2009 at http://www.illinois.gov/elrb/

6. However, in *Marion Community School Corporation v. Marion Teachers Association*, 873 N.E.2d 605 (Ind. App. 2007), the Indiana Court of Appeals upheld

an arbitrator's award for attorney's fees for the prevailing union even though there was no provision for attorney's fees in the contract. In addition, the arbitrators' requirement that the school district issue an apology to the grievant in an effort to make the grievant whole for potential loss to his reputation was upheld. The Court write, "an apology teaches the School Corporation to follow the Agreement in the future and also not to make derogatory comments in the newspaper. Indiana law provides an arbitrator with the broad remedial authority to make such an award" (610).

7. *Marion Community School Corporation v. Marion Teachers Association*, 873 N.E.2d 605 (Ind. App. 2007).

8. For example, the City of Oswego, New York violated past practice when it unilaterally prohibited firefighters from washing and waxing their private vehicles in City fire stations during work time. The New York Public Employment Relations Board found that the Fire Chief's awareness and acceptance/acquiescence of the practice established a past practice that required bargaining if a change in the practice is sought. *City of Oswego Firefighters Association, IAFF, Local 2701 and City of Oswego*, U-27221, 5/20/08.

9. See, *Collier Insulated Wire*, 192 N.L.R.B. 837 (1971).

10. Deborah M. Kolb, *The mediators* (Cambridge, MA: MIT Press, 1983): 27.

11. Ibid. See pages 23–28 for an interesting discussion of a mediator as a dealmaker.

12. *Antonio Jenkins and United Federation of Teachers, Local 2, AFT, AFL-CIO and Board of Education of the City School District of the City of New York*, U-26822, 4/3/08.

13. David A. Lax and James K. Sebenius, *3D negotiations: Powerful tools to change the game in your most important deals* (Cambridge, MA: Harvard Business School Press, 2006): 37.

14. Roger Fisher and William Ury, *Getting to yes: Negotiating agreement without giving in* (New York: Penguin Books, 1981): xi.

15. Ibid. 10.

16. Ibid. 6.

17. Ibid. 38.

18. Ibid. 54.

19. "If they have made an unreasonable proposal or attack you regard as unjustified, the best thing to do may be to sit there and not say a word" (Ibid. 117).

20. Ibid. 104.

21. Richard E. Maurer, *Managing conflict: Tactics for school administrators* (Boston: Allyn and Bacon, 1991): 113.

22. Roger Fisher and Scott Brown, *Getting together: Building relationships as we negotiate* (New York: Penguin Books, 1988).

23. Ibid. 38.

24. Ibid. "The high moral content of the guidelines is a bonus."

25. Ibid. 8.

26. Ibid. 54.

27. Ibid. 86.

28. Ibid. 109–11.

29. Ibid. 21.

30. Ibid. 192.

31. Ibid. 5.

32. William G. Keane, *Win win or else: Collective bargaining in an age of public discontent.* (Thousand Oaks, CA: Corwin Press, Inc., 1996): 36.

33. Ibid. 32.

Chapter 5

Professionalism and Unionism

> Only professionals are *expected* to act in the public interest, to create a
> calculus that balances self-and-civic interest.[1]

For some, the words professional and union member do not fit easily together. Teachers consider themselves to be professionals,[2] and public education is the most heavily unionized occupation in the United States.[3] Teacher unionism and professionalism have had a peculiar and tenuous relationship. Schuman writes the following of this conundrum: "Teachers want to be respected, want to be thought of as professionals, yet are members of strong labor unions."[4] While they consider themselves professionals, they want the protection that comes from being a member of a union. How the tenets of unionization and professional notions of teaching coexist is an issue with which many educators as well as teacher unions have struggled. "Historically, professionalism has been defined in ways that are detrimental to union organization."[5]

The influence of collective bargaining and unions and their impact on teachers and schools is salient in a time of high stakes accountability and policy making. Too little is known about the impact of these two forces on public education.[6] DeMitchell and Barton in their study of principals', teachers', and union building representatives' perceptions of reform and collective bargaining posed the following tentative conclusion: "Although the rise of unions and collective bargaining was built on a foundation of self-interest, that self-interest may not extend to professional activities . . . Teachers may not see unions as being related to activities that are at the core teaching."[7]

The concern about the impact of the industrial labor model on teaching leads to the issue—does collective bargaining, the work of unions, promote "a conception of teaching as labor rather than as professional work."[8] How do teachers reconcile the seemingly disparate, even contradictory roles of member of a learned profession and union member? According to Cooper and Liotta the conundrum is that while "teachers in many communities are union members, they still see themselves and their work as primarily professional—helping children to learn."[9]

> On the one hand, there are members of the organization who identify with a professional image and who strive to create a teacher organization that will affirm this professional image. On the other hand there are members whose desire to perceive themselves, and to be perceived by others, as professionals is less of an imperative.[10]

THE CONUNDRUM: THE ROLE OF THE UNION

Unionism is predicated upon serving the needs of its members. Teachers under collective bargaining moved from being spoken for by school administrators and board of education to representing their interests through an exclusive representative—the union. Those needs, commonly called bread-and-butter, are wages, benefits, terms and conditions of employment including security. At the advent of collective bargaining "[t]eachers wanted higher salaries and better benefits, not necessarily a higher standard of respect."[11] The job of the union is to "get" those things for its members. "Unions provide a collective voice that seeks to enhance and secure the social and economic wellbeing of its members."[12]

However, as Kerchner and Mitchell note, the legitimation of unions pursuing teacher economic interests through collective bargaining "has aroused public suspicion that teachers no longer speak for the public interest of schools or represent the real needs of children."[13] If teachers don't, which professional does?

Teachers look to their union for protection from those outside their classroom, primarily administrators and to some degree parents. There is an old saying in labor relations that, "administrators always get the union they deserve." In other words, if administrators are excessively intrusive, arbitrary, and/or capricious in their decision making, employees will feel the need for the protection a union provides.

The findings of the DeMitchell and Cobb study underscore this point. Teachers who responded to their survey question, "without a union school administrators would diminish my professional decision making", agreed or strongly agreed with this statement by a margin of 55.3 percent to 30.1 percent strongly disagreeing or disagreeing with it.[14] Teachers in this study believe they need to be protected from administrators. Yet, 64 percent of these respondents believe that their professional activities are enhanced through collegial relationships with administrators.[15]

Similarly, more respondents in the study agreed or strongly agreed (81.4 percent versus 9.8 percent who strongly disagreed or disagreed) "I am better off as a professional with a union contract than without a union contract." However, it is interesting to note that union leaders and rank and file members significantly disagreed on the question with union leaders more strongly agreeing than the rank and file members.[16]

Teachers in this study believe that a union protects them from administrators, that they are better off with a contract, yet believe that their professional activities are enhanced through collegial relations with these same administrators. As the title of the DeMitchell and Cobb study states, the relationship between union and profession is tangled.

In her study of union leaders, Poole, discusses what she calls the "paradox" of self-interest and educational interest. She writes, "Union leaders have a belief system that values quality public education for its own sake because it is right for children and right for society; however, they also support quality public education because it provides the means to support the union and its members."[17] A union leader in her study melded the pursuit of the economic welfare of its members with educational quality in the following way:

> The union can create a good environment for children by and after protecting the teachers. And I guess that boils down to [economic welfare] . . . That trickles down to children.. Because if your teachers are hurting, then your children are going to hurt. If you have teachers who are happy and are satisfied with their union, and have a reasonable wage to live comfortably, and don't have to worry about whether their job is going to be there next year or not, then I think you're going to have a better educational environment for the children.[18]

In other words, what is good for teachers is good for children, and it is best to take care of teachers first, which will in turn take care of children. This view places teachers at the core of education. Student wellbeing flows from teacher wellbeing, ostensibly secured through bargaining. Is this position akin to saying that what is best for physicians "trickles down" to what is best for patients?

The union's function is legally and psychologically distanced from the responsibility for the institution of education[19] Even though both the NEA and the AFT have stressed that teaching is a profession, their emphasis has been on attaining material benefits such as higher wages and better health insurance. The importance of this central function of the union cannot be understated.

The Rand study conducted by McDonnell and Pascal found that "union efforts to obtain status benefits such as increased participation in school-site decision making often engenders teacher suspicion and a feeling that the union is 'falling down on the job.'"[20] And, that until a "union obtains these bread-and-butter items, movement toward greater professionalism is not likely."[21] Clearly, teachers expect their union to take care of business first, and the first business of a union is to secure the material benefits of their employment. Professionalism may ride in the backseat with bread-and-butter riding upfront driving the car.

DeMitchell and Cobb's research underscores this point. They posed the following statement: "Unions pursue the bread and butter issues of wages, benefits, and security over professional issues." Sixty-seven percent of the respondents agree or strongly agree with the proposition. Only 2.9 percent marked strongly disagree.[22] The researchers write, "This is not surprising because this is what unions do in the collective bargaining process—pursue the self-interests of the members. It also underscores the tension between the work of unions and the goals of professionals."[23]

But, interestingly, the response to another question on self- interest and professional interests points to the tangled view that teachers have regarding the two roles. Just over 38 percent (38.4 percent) agree or strongly agree with the statement "If I had to choose, I would prefer that the contract protect my self-interest (e.g., salary) over my professional interests (e.g., pedagogy)." Almost a third (32.7 percent) sought the safe harbor of Neutral while just under 29 percent (28.7 percent) strongly disagree or disagree with the statement.[24] Does the large neutral response reflect a tension between the preferred response—protect my professional interests—and the reality based response—protect my self-interests?

Bob Chase, the former president of the NEA, pursued a policy of reinventing the union. Speaking to the local NEA leadership in Florida about the union's role in achieving school quality, one union member stated, "Your job isn't to look out for the children; your job is to look out for me!"[25] This succinct statement captures the basic role of a union—to look out for the welfare of its members. Unions protect and represent their members.

This perception appears to state that one can either be a union member pursuing collective self-interests or one can be a professional who pursues the interests of patients, clients, or students. However, Urbanski finds the dichotomy to be false writing, "to achieve a more genuine profession, teachers themselves will have to reject the phony choices between compensation and dedication, between unionism and professionalism, and between equity and excellence."[26] DeMitchell and Cobb were not so sure that this dichotomy is so easily resolved. Susan Moore Johnson captured this position of tension some two decades earlier to the DeMitchell and Cobb study writing, "The school site is a place where teachers' values rather than union values prevail."[27]

The table is set. On one side is the union member pursuing his or her self-interest through a collectively bargained contract. On the other side of the table is the professional educator who serves the best interests of the students. Or, do they sit on the same side of the table? The DeMitchell and Cobb studies (2006 & 2007) will be reviewed after the discussion on professionalism to gain a perspective on how teachers may be reconciling or attempting to reconcile these two roles.

THE CONUNDRUM OF THE ROLE
OF THE PROFESSIONAL

What does it mean to be a professional? Casey states that professionalism is essentially a "contested concept."[28] The term is used loosely in everyday life. Helterbran notes that the general practice is to use the term professional "as both a position for which someone is paid and the quality of the performance of one's job."[29] This chapter focuses are on neither of those conceptions of professionals—the professional athlete versus the amateur athlete or the cab driver who treats you in a professional manner and gets you directly to your destination quickly and in one piece. Instead, this chapter will focus on the member of a learned profession.

Professional educators should obviously be paid as opposed to volunteering their services, they should treat students, parents, and fellow educators, including administrators in a respectful professional manner, and they should act with integrity,[30] we should also strive for the higher standard of a member of a learned profession which holds service to the other—the individual or individuals dependent upon the service being rendered—as the highest ideal. This chapter will use the term professional to mean a member of a learned profession.

Professionalism is built around expert knowledge, usually gained through extensive education and training.[31] Professional work is complex and non-routine. It involves a standard of practice recognized and adhered to by the practitioners but applied in varying contexts. The standards are enforced by the professional organization, typically through an internal code of ethics.[32] Professionals exercise judgment within the accepted standards in the best interest of the client or others. Because judgment must be used in applying professional knowledge to meet client's needs, that knowledge cannot be easily reduced to rules or prescriptions.

Further divorcing industrial unionism from professional practice is the understanding and accepted notion that it is exercised for the good of the public, whereas, unionism protects the self-interest of its members.

"Professionals are obligated to do whatever is best for the client, not what is easiest. Most expedient, or even what the client himself or herself might want."[33] Similarly, William J. Goode argued that one of the two core principles of professionalism is a "service orientation."[34] The second is a specialized body of knowledge gained through extended study.

Specific to education and professionalism, the National Board for Professional Teaching Standards has identified five core propositions: (1) teachers are committed to students and their learning, (2) teachers know the subjects they teach and how to teach those subjects to students, (3) teachers are responsible for managing and monitoring student learning, (4) teachers think systematically about their practice and learn from experience, and (5) teachers are members of learning communities.[35] These five propositions are supported by the assumptions that professionalism is predicated upon the following:

> [A] body of specialized, expert knowledge together with a code of ethics emphasizing service to clients. The knowledge base typically provides substantial, but not complete, guidance for professional practice. Professionals possess expert knowledge, but often confront unique, problematic situations that do not lend themselves to formulaic solutions. Professionals must cultivate the ability to cope with the unexpected and act wisely in the face of uncertainty. . . . [P]rofessionals . . . pursue an ethic of service and . . . employ special knowledge and expertise in the interests of their clients.[36]

Echoing the National Board, Linda Darling-Hammond offered the following three principles of professionalism:

1. Knowledge is the basis for permission to practice and for decisions that are made with respect to the unique needs of clients.
2. The practitioner pledges his [/her] first concern of welfare to the client.
3. The profession assumes collective responsibility for the definition, transmittal, and enforcement of professional standards of practice and ethics.[37]

Professionalism holds a special place for teachers. For example, in a follow up study on teachers' perceptions of their academic freedom,[38] Fries, Connelly, and DeMitchell conducted focus group research with public school teachers.[39] The participants were given a scenario on academic freedom that served as a springboard for the discussion. Higher education considers academic freedom to be a constitutionally based freedom. The teachers in this qualitative study did not adopt that legal foundation for academic freedom. Instead, the first theme that emerged from the data was professionalism defines academic freedom.

The teacher participants consistently referred to professionalism when discussing the contours of their academic freedom. Professionalism to them was
less of a right and more of a responsibility. The teachers couched their analysis
of academic freedom in terms of their professional relationship to the students.

The term professional is not one that is associated with jurisprudence
on academic freedom in either higher education or academic freedom in
the public schools. Professionalism is a wider concept than free speech in
the schools. "Free speech as the touchstone for academic freedom focuses
on the rights of the teacher/professor, whereas academic freedom based on
professionalism is based on the responsibilities owed to the recipient of the
professional activity (e.g., instruction)."[40] It is noteworthy that these teachers
grounded their sense of academic freedom on the bedrock of the professional
responsibility that they owe their students.

THE FIT IN TWO PARTS

As stated above, DeMitchell and Cobb conducted a single study on the fit
between union membership and a member of a profession but reported their
findings in two articles. The two studies will be reviewed. The overarching
question was, "[Are] teacher unions and collective bargaining compatible
with teacher perceptions of professionalism."[41] The following specific questions focused the research.

1. Do union activities support the professionalism of its members?
2. Does a collectively bargained contract support the professional activities
   of teachers?
3. Is there a difference between the union leaders' perceptions and the perceptions of the rank-and-file members with regard to professionalism?

The survey included twenty-four Likert-style items that asked respondents their level of agreement with a variety of statements relative to their
perceptions of the teaching profession and teacher unions.[42] The items were
developed to discern respondents' understanding of how they reconcile the
apparent contradiction of the role of unions predicated on furthering their
self-interest and their role as a professional grounded in service to the student
(e.g., *professionalism is compatible with union activity.*).

In particular, items were constructed around seven categories: (1) the
intersection of professionalism and unionism, (2) the legacy of the industrial union, (3) the tension between self-interest and professional interests
which focus on an ethic of care to one whom receives the professional

service, (4) the separation of educators into us and them, (5) the elements of professional work, (6) the intersection of teaching and the contract, and (7) serving the professional needs of teachers.

The surveys were sent to randomly selected schools in states that have public sector collective bargaining laws. One hundred and three teachers responded.

The second part of the research asks teachers to respond to two prompts.[43] These prompts seek to gather more in-depth knowledge about teachers' perceptions of professionalism and the role of the union by asking whether unions support or harm professionalism. This part is an extension of the quantitative method of the first part of the study utilizing a quasi-quantitative method designed to gain greater depth of understanding of the data. While it uses qualitative analytical tools, it is not, strictly speaking, a qualitative design. The two prompts were: *Unions support professionalism in the following ways*: and *Unions harm professionalism in the following ways*.

The respondents were given the following definition of professionalism in an effort to provide clarity and consistency in responses.

"For purposes of this survey, please use the following definition of professionalism or professional work:

- Professionalism involves the use of expert knowledge gained through extended study
- Professionalism involves the use of expert knowledge in unique and problematic situations.
- Professionalism is bounded by a code of ethics that emphasizes service to a client/student.
- Professional work is essentially intellectual and varied.
- Professional work requires the autonomy to control one's work.
- Professional work is not routine work."[44]

Only a few of the more salient findings for this chapter will be reported here leaving the reader to go to the original if greater depth of understanding is warranted. Unless otherwise noted, the likert scale is one (1) is strongly disagree to five (5) strongly agree. The larger the mean the larger the agreement with the statement.

- The teachers consider their union to be a professional organization rather than a traditional industrial union ($M = 3.80$).[45] However, almost one-third (32.3 percent) disagree/strongly disagree that hardball labor tactics like strikes conflict with their sense of professionalism.[46] In other words, the teachers belong to a professional association not a labor union but almost one-third saw no conflict when this professional association acts like an industrial union.

- Unions are predicated upon serving the self-interests of its members. Yet, less than half of the respondents in this research (42.5 percent) agree or strongly agree with the proposition. *(M* = 3.10). Why would teachers not acknowledge this essential truth?

The respondents seemed similarly conflicted about the role of the union protecting the interests of the students *(M* = 3.15) and the interests of the public *(M* = 3.01).[47] These latter two statements are more consistent with the role of professionalism, protecting the "other" over self. In an interesting twist, elementary school teachers' responses were significantly different than middle and high school teachers. The elementary school teachers had a mean of 2.63 disagreeing with the statement that unions protect the interests of the public while middle *(M* = 3.21) and high school teachers *(M* = 3.32) agree with the statement. Elementary school teachers, on this question, appear to hold the more traditional view that a union is not created to further the public good.

This question tends to lay bare the issue of unionism versus professionalism. If unions do not protect the public's interests, can teachers lay legitimate claim to being part of a true profession since teachers tend to find unionism and professionalism to be compatible? Does the teacher's apparent conflicted responses reflect this tension between legitimate roles, union member and professional, without finding a satisfactory resolution?

- The section of the instrument on Teaching and the Contract goes to the heart of professionalism and unionism. Five questions sought to understand how the contract supports or inhibits teaching, the core professional activity. Teachers believe that the contract protects their professional activities *(M* = 3.77) but the mean response to the statement that the contract fosters quality teaching is on the other side of neutral *(M* = 2.72).[48] Only 21.8 percent agree or strongly agree with the statement. However, almost one-third (31.8 percent) take refuge in the neutral response. Does this mean that they do not know what impact the contract has on their teaching or are they uncomfortable with their conclusion and seek not to disclose it?

While the teachers believe that the contract supports their ability to make independent decisions regarding their teaching *(M* = 3.50), they also believe that the artistic/creative elements of teaching *(M* = 2.66) cannot be addressed in the contract nor can quality teaching be standardized into a contract *(M* = 2.45).[49] "Teachers in this study perceive that teaching may be too complex to fit neatly into the strictures of collective bargaining."[50] The responses to this section underscore how tangled the relationship is between union member and member of a learned profession. The contract, according to the responding teachers, supports professional decision making but it does not seem to support quality teaching.

DeMitchell and Cobb conclude:

> Teachers are professionals. How their professionalism meshes with union membership and bargained contracts is tangled. The contract protects their professionalism in the abstract but may not protect it in concrete ways. They want the union and the contract to fit into their professional lives but may have not buffed those edges or possibly figured out a way to buff those ragged edges that allow for a neat fit between professional activity and union membership. Could it be that unions and contracts protect teachers' sense of professionalism but other mechanisms enhance and support the professional activities of teaching?[51]

Short Answer

A total of seventy-seven teachers responded to the prompts of harm and support.[52] Most responded to both prompts, but not all did. All responses were transcribed and an iterative process of reviewing each response was conducted. Categories of responses were developed and then refined several times. Three themes emerged from the support prompt and four themes emerged from the harm prompt. The theme of protection was found in both prompts but with opposite meanings.

Unions Support Professionalism in the Following Ways

A total of seventy-one teachers responded to this prompt. There was a strong sense in some of the responses of harbored past wrongs. Specific resentments were directed at administrators, whether past or present administrators is unknown. For example, an elementary school teacher wrote, *"Provide support to abused teachers (those unfairly reprimanded)"*, and a high school teacher stated, *"They protect my legal right from being trampled"*.[53]

DeMitchell and Cobb also found that a second use of language in this prompt that stands out is the unilateral power of the union and the checking power of the union on administrative action. Power words describing unions include: protect, secure, support, provide, ensure, and guarantee. At times the impression from the response is that the union is exercising unilateral power. For example, an elementary school teacher states that the union *"provides days for inservice and professional development."*[54] Obviously, unions cannot provide inservice and professional development days unilaterally.

The workdays are not theirs to give. However, for these teachers, including past and present union leaders, these conditions of employment would not be possible without the union. In other words, these teachers may question whether the school district would support these activities.

However, in their first study, DeMitchell and Cobb posed this question to the same respondents, "I look to the union and not to the school district to meet my professional inservice needs." Eighty-three percent (83.5 percent) strongly disagree or disagree with the statement. Only four respondents agree or strongly agree with the statement.[55] Once again, the roles of the professional and the union member are tangled.

Three themes emerged from the data; protection, advocacy, and support.

Protection

The major thrust of this theme is that teachers would be in deep trouble without the union protecting them from administrators who are often characterized as mean, venal, and petty. For example, teachers write:

- *"I feel that teachers would be taken advantage of by administrators in their district if not protected by our union"* (elementary school teacher, union office holder).
- *"Protect you from inept administrators and Protect teachers from the whims of administrators"* (elementary school teacher).
- *"The best teachers are often a threat"* (middle school teacher).
- *"Protection from arbitrary actions by incompetent administrators who stifle the creative professionalism possible in our career"* (high school teacher, union office holder).[56]

These written responses are consistent with the responses to a question in the section The Profession and the Union ("Without a union school administrators would diminish my professional decision making.") The mean was 3.49 with 55.3 percent agreeing or strongly agreeing that the union protects teachers from administrators.[57]

Advocacy

The theme of advocacy includes how the contract attracts, retains, and frees up teachers. "A number of these comments describe a powerful union that 'assures' and 'allows' teachers to perform their professional duties without interference from administrators. The comments tend to give the impression that the union is not just a restraint on administrative action but that it may compel administrative action. These comments describe a proactive union and not a reactive union."[58] These elements focus on one of the major duties of the union, bargaining.

Another related concept is that unions enhance teaching through their advocacy that teaching is a profession. The comments on the contract as advocate include: *"bargains for teachers to be paid like they are professionals"* (elementary school); *"guarantees competitive wages, etc. to keep good individuals in this profession"* (middle school teacher, union office holder); *"Union contract speaks to a variety of important conditions that make professionalism prosper"* (high school teacher, union office holder); and a middle school teacher provides a good summary, *"Allow[s] teachers to pursue their profession with less concern for contractual issues, which they would otherwise dedicate valuable time pursuing if they negotiated individually."*[59]

The concept of enhancing teaching within the advocacy theme includes such comments as: *"In this era of 'scripted teaching,' I am assured my right to teach students in creative & effective ways"* (elementary school, union office holder) and *"My union allows me to try things without long term censure from my administrators"* (middle school teacher, union office holder).[60]

This sub-theme appears to reconcile the two role of professional and union member because it is the union that supports the professional work of the teacher. However, if the major work of unions is the bargaining and management of the contract, how is the following statement from the quantitative portion reconciled with this sub-theme? The statement reads, "The artistic/creative elements of teaching can be addressed in a contract." The mean is 2.66 (disagreeing) with only 26.8 percent agreeing or strongly agreeing with the statement.[61] Furthermore, just over 61 percent of the respondents strongly disagreed or disagreed with the following proposition, "If I had a professional issue/question, unrelated to the contract, I would first turn to the union for assistance."[62]

The findings of the two parts of the study are tangled and not straightforward. Is advocacy for an external audience while the search for support for professional practice turns inward to the school and administrators?

Support

The last theme concerns inservice days and professional development. The respondents credit the union with securing time for these important pursuits. There are a total of 14 (eight elementary school teachers, four middle school teachers, and two high school teachers) responses constituting 20 percent of the total written comments. Offering workshops, peer collaboration, promoting activities to support best practices, encouraging professional development, and *"require[ing] professional development as part of the contract"* (high school teacher) are cited as examples of how unions support professionalism.[63]

The teachers who responded to this prompt of support, believe that not only is union membership compatible with professionalism but that it is associated with providing a professional service to students.[64] The responses comprising these three themes reflect the quantitative responses that the teachers need the protection of the union and that they are better off working under a union contract than working without a contract.

Unions Harm Professionalism in the Following Ways

A total of 23 (seven union office holders) elementary school teachers, 23 middle school teachers (four union office holders), and 15 high school teachers (five union office holders) responded to this prompt. The views expressed are not as hard-edged as some of the comments cited above. While there are some frustrated commentators, the comments, by-and-large, do not contain the same emotional content of personal wrongs. The comments appear to be more disagreements with and lamentations about the current state of affairs. However, one middle school teacher's comments may have captured the tone of the most strident criticisms of unions and summed up for many their concerns about unions. The middle school teacher wrote in the prompt for how unions support professionalism, *"Unions are the antithesis of professionalism!"*[65]

Four themes emerge from the analysis—blind protection, the work of unions, divisiveness, and the union label.

Blind Protection

The issue of protection was the strongest theme of how unions support professionalism.[66] It is also the strongest theme of how unions harm professionalism. Clearly the issue of union protection is central to many teachers and it is also a cause of great concern for many other teachers. Protection appears to be a double-edged sword: the union provides needed protection from the powerful and sometimes less than professional administrators versus protection of incompetent teachers, which demeans the profession.[67] Protection of the least capable teacher is a challenge for unions because most teachers are "troubled by the presence of incompetent teachers in their school building."[68]

For some, union protection is almost an unthinking genuflection of protection of the least worthy, while for others the protection of a union member is important for all teachers regardless of the fitness of the individual. One high school union leader wrote of this conundrum for unions, *"Sometimes we have to support people who we think are poor teachers."* An elementary school teacher and union office holder stated, *"Automatically defending teachers whether they are right or wrong."* However, one high school teacher placed the blame on administrators for the retention of incompetent teachers writing, *"If administrators would do their jobs there has always been ways provided in contracts to help these teachers or eventually remove them."*[69]

Work of the Union

Two sub themes comprise this theme: union activities (*"Unions focus on money, making teachers seem self-serving and unprofessional."*)[70] and pressure to conform (*"Also, if the union member does not wish to participate in certain activities, such as refusing to do activities after the school day, other staff members will sometimes try to apply pressure to conform"*).[71] The larger connection of the two sub themes is found in an elementary school teacher's response: *"[The union] totally disregards the work ethic teachers choose to put into their job and instead places trivial issue sat the forefront of their day-to-day business."*[72] This comment incorporates the pressure to conform—the disregard of the effort teachers put into their job—and what the teacher chooses is immaterial if it does not fit the viewpoint of the union on what should be done as part of the work. It also includes union activities, although not specified, that supercede what teachers want to do. This is opposite to the positive theme of advocacy discussed above.

Divisiveness

Some of the comments are purely descriptive—*"Creates a 'them' and 'us' atmosphere"* (middle school teacher), while some respondents see conflict in the divisiveness—*"Often promotes an antagonistic relationship between teachers and administrators and school board"* (middle school teacher) and *"Interfere w/ positive interactions between admin & teachers" "Create adversarial atmosphere"* (high school teacher, union office holder).[73] Koppich notes this outcome when she writes, "[o]n the one hand, industrial-style collective bargaining gave teachers a voice and influence when they had none. . . . On the other hand, industrial unionism circumscribed teaching and created a kind of professional chasm between teachers and administrators."[74]

Interestingly, the responses to the survey instrument paint a different picture. The responses to the statement "Unionization institutionalizes conflict between teachers and school administrators" can be separated in the following manner: 45.8 percent (strongly disagree/disagree), 29.2 percent (neutral), and 25 percent (agree/strongly disagree). And, the same analysis can be applied to "The contract separates educators into us (teachers) and them (administrators): 30.4 percent (strongly disagree/disagree), 22.5 percent (neutral), and 47 percent (agree/strongly agree).[75] The respondents establishing this theme clearly must be in the minority of the total respondents. However, it is striking that there are large neutral responses.

The responses to these two questions are consistent with the other in this subset of Us and Them. Sixty-four percent of the respondents agreed or strongly agreed that their professional activities are enhanced through collegial relationships with administrators.[76]

The Union Label

The union label theme refers to a belief that association with a union harms professionalism in the eyes of teachers and possibly more importantly in the eyes of the public, which one can argue, confers the honorific of professionalism. One elementary school teacher stated *"just the paradigm of 'union' causes hostility."* A middle school teacher wrote, *"Unions harm professionalism in the negative feelings/opinions that some have of unions."* Another elementary school teacher may have summed up this theme with the comment *"I don't hold banners/pickets . . . it's not what I do if it's for self interest."* [77]

If the union label means the teacher association acts like its predecessor the industrial union, the response to the following statement supports this theme of harm, "Hardball labor tactics, such as work-to-rule or strikes, associated with industrial unions conflict with my sense of professionalism." Just over half of the respondents (56.2 percent) agreed or strongly agreed with the statement.[78] Union leaders and rank-and-file members had a significant difference on this question ($p = .002$) with union leaders having a mean of 2.83 meaning that hardball tactics do not conflict with their sense of professionalism and non-leaders having a mean on the other side of neutral of 3.61.[79] Non-union leaders believe that hardball tactics conflict with their sense of professionalism, while union leaders hold an opposite viewpoint.

The teachers in this study (reported as separate articles) are not monolithic in their understanding and approach to this potential conflict. Teachers want the protection of a union and a collectively bargained contract. They, however, note that there are limits to what the contract and the union can do to support their professional activities, especially when it comes to bargaining the professional contours of teaching. Union leaders and non-leaders differ significantly on several specific issues. However, they appear to be united as to whether they are better off with a union and a contract. "While their responses as to how unionism and professionalism fit together may be tangled, they are clear that ambiguity is preferable to working without a union and a collective bargaining contract."[80]

Teachers struggle for ways to find a fit between their union membership, with its emphasis on pursuing self-interest, with their possibly their greater identification as a professional with service in the best interests of the other: the student, the patient, or the client. In an essay critical of unions and professional responsibilities, Terry Moe concludes, "The education system is not a jobs program. It does not exist for the benefit of the adults who run it. It exists to educate children."[81] Unions and their members face the challenge of how to emphasize teacher professional responsibilities to students without predicating those responsibilities on securing their self-interests first. The primacy of the contract in securing teacher interests is an unlikely vehicle for securing the needs of students. The prohibition of bargaining policy constructs this reach of bargaining into classroom products.

Ronald Henderson, the Director of the Research Department at the NEA underscores this point. He writes, "Collective bargaining has been too weak and too narrow to change the basic conditions that prevent teaching from becoming a profession on par with other vital functions in society."[82] If not through collective bargaining, the major work of a union, what can the union do to secure, maintain, and augment their member's professional work and professional standing? Unions and bargaining are structured to emphasize the labor aspect of employment, thus, making unionism and professionalism a challenging fit.

NOTES

1. Charles T. Kerchner and Douglas E. Mitchell, *The changing idea of a teachers' union* (Philadelphia: Falmer Press, 1988): 227.

2. Todd A. DeMitchell and Casey D. Cobb, "Teachers: Their union and their profession. A tangled relationship," *Education Law Reporter* 212 (2006): 1–20. On a five-point Likert type scale (1= strongly disagree to 5=strongly agree) teachers had a mean of 4.91 on the question "Teaching is a profession" p. 11.

3. Terry M. Moe writes, "the largest, most powerful union in the country is not the Teamsters or the United Auto Workers, but the National Education Association." *A union by any other name*, EDUCATION NEXT (2001). Site visited June 15, 2007 at www.educationnext.org/20013/38moe.html.

4. David Schuman, *American schools, american teachers: Issues and perspectives* (Boston: Pearson, 2004): 89.

5. Charles Taylor Kerchner and Krista D. Caufman, "Lurching toward professionalism: the saga of teacher unionism," in *The Elementary School Journal* 96 (1995): 110.

6. Michael Kirst likened our understanding of the role unions play in policy making as a "dark continent." In Ann Bradley, *Education's "dark continent," education week* (December 4, 1996): 25; Charles Taylor Kerchner, Julia E. Koppich, and Joseph G. Weeres, *United mind workers: Unions and teaching in the knowledge society* (San Francisco: Jossey-Bass Publishers, 1997), referred to unions as "the blind spot on the radar scope of educational reform" (xi); Jane Hannaway and Andrew J. Rotherham, *Collective bargaining in education: Negotiating change in today's schools* (Cambridge, MA: Harvard Education Press, 2006), there is a "profound lack of relevant data, research, and analysis" on the role of collective bargaining and reform (1).

7. Todd A. DeMitchell and Richard W. Barton, "Collective bargaining and its impact on local educational reform efforts." *Educational Policy* 10 (1996): 375.

8. Nina Bascia, *Unions in teachers' professional lives: Social, intellectual, and practical concerns* (New York: Teachers College Press, 1994): 3.

9. Bruce S. Cooper and Marie-Elena Liotta, "Urban teachers unions face their future: the dilemmas of organizational maturity" in *Education and Urban Society* 34, 2001): 109.

10. Wendy L. Poole, "The construction of teachers' paradoxical interests by teacher union leaders," in *American Educational Research Journal* (2001): 101–102.

11. William A. Streshly and Todd A. DeMitchell, *Teacher unions and TQE: Building quality labor relations* (Thousand Oaks, CA: Corwin Press, Inc, 1994): 10.

12. Todd A. DeMitchell and Casey D. Cobb, Commentary "The Professional and the Union Member: A Tangled Fit," *Teachers College Record* (December 12, 2007). Http://www.trecord.org/content.asp?ContentId=14854 ID 14854.

13. Kerchner and Mitchell, *supra* note 1, 239.

14. DeMitchell and Cobb, *supra* note 2, 11. There is a significant difference between the responses of union leaders and members. Union officers had a mean of 4.21, above 4.00 agree while non-officers had a mean of 3.08 just above neutral.

15. Ibid. 15.

16. Ibid. 18.

17. Poole, *supra* note 10, 117.

18. Ibid. 107–108.

19. Kerchner and Mitchell, *supra* note 1.

20. Lorraine M. McDonnell and Anthony Pascal, *Teacher unions and educational reform* (Santa Monica, CA: Rand, April 1988): 53.

21. Ibid.

22. DeMitchell and Cobb, *supra* note 2, 16.

23. Ibid.

24. Ibid. 13.

25. Bob Chase, The new NEA: Reinventing teacher unions for a new era. Remarks before the National Press Club. Washington, DC (February 7 1997). Site accessed August 9, 1997 at http://www.nea.org.

26. Adam Urbanski, "Improving student achievement through labor-management collaboration in urban school districts." *Education Policy* 17 (2003): 507.

27. Susan Moore Johnson, "Teacher unions in schools: Authority and accommodation," in *Harvard Educational Review* 53 (1983): 325.

28. Leo Casey, "The educational value of democratic voice: A defense of collective bargaining in american education," in Jane Hannaway and Andrew J. Rotherham, *Collective bargaining in education: Negotiating change in today's schools* (Cambridge, MA: Harvard Education Press, 2006): 189.

29. Valeri R. Helterbran, "Professionalism: Teachers taking the reins," *The Clearing House* 81 (2008): 124.

30. Helterbran, *supra*, writes that anecdotal responses to her query about what contributes to teacher professionalism, received some of the following responses; "doing my job, loving to be around children, dressing well. Doing my own lesson plans, not calling in sick on professional development days, and providing fun, engaging activities for my students" (124).

31. Eliot Freidson, *Profession of medicine* (Chicago: University of Chicago Press, 1988).

32. Bernard Barber, "Some problems in the sociology of professions," *Daedalus* 92 (1963): 669–88.

33. Linda Darling-Hammond, "Accountability for professional practice," In *Teachers College Record* 91 (1989): 67.

34. William J. Goode, "Encroachment, charlatanism, and the emerging profession: psychology, medicine, and sociology" in *American Sociological Review* 25 (1960): 903.

35. National Board of Professional Teaching Standards. What teachers should know and be able to do: The five core propositions of the National Board. Site visited November 2, 2003, www.nbts.org/about/coreprops.cfm#introfcp, 3–4.

36. Ibid. 6.

37. Darling-Hammond. *supra* note 33, 67.

38. Todd A. DeMitchell and Vincent J. Connelly, "Academic freedom and the public school teacher: An exploratory study of perceptions, policy and the law" in *Brigham Young University Education and Law Journal* 207 (2007): 83–117.

39. Kim Fries, Vincent J. Connelly, and Todd A. DeMitchell, "Academic Freedom in the Public K-12 Classroom: Professional Responsibility or Constitutional Right? A Conversation with Teachers," in *Education Law Reporter*, 227 (2008): 505–24.

40. Ibid. 518.

41. DeMitchell and Cobb, *supra* note 2, 19.

42. The five point scale directed the respondents to select one of the following responses to the statement: 1=strongly disagree, 2=disagree, 3=neutral, 4=agree, and 5=strongly agree. The higher the mean the higher the agreement with the statement.

43. Todd A. DeMitchell and Casey D. Cobb, "Teacher as union member and teacher as professional: The voice of the teacher" in *Education Law Reporter* 220 (2007): 25–38.

44. Ibid. 28.

45. DeMitchell and Cobb, *supra* note 2, 13. It is interesting to note that the National Education Association has been classified as a union since 1976 by the Bureau of Labor Statistics and the Internal Revenue Service, yet one would be hard pressed to find an NEA affiliate that used the term union in its title.

46. Ibid. 12–13. Union leaders differed from non-union leaders in which the former tended to find little conflict between hardball tactics and professionalism while the latter found hardball tactics troubling.

47. Ibid. 13.

48. Ibid. 18. Union leaders ($M = 3.34$) responses are significantly different ($p = .002$) from non-leaders ($M = 2.40$). There is a real disconnect between the two groups of teachers on the influence of the contract on quality teaching—the heart of the professional activity of teachers.

49. Ibid.

50. Ibid. 17.

51. Ibid. 20.

52. DeMitchell and Cobb, *supra* note 43, the total of 77 responses included 33 elementary school, 26 middle school, and 18 high school teachers, p. 31.

53. Ibid.

54. Ibid.

55. DeMitchell and Cobb, *supra note* 2, 18. The mean for this statement is 2.08, the lowest mean in the study.

56. DeMitchell and Cobb, *supra* note 43, 32.

57. DeMitchell and Cobb, *supra note* 2, 11.

58. DeMitchell and Cobb, *supra* note 43, 33.

59. Ibid. 32.

60. Ibid.

61. DeMitchell and Cobb, *supra note* 2, 18.

62. Ibid. p. 18, $M = 2.54$. Further confounding the issue, as stated above, on the statement the teacher looks first to the union rather than the school district to meet their inservice needs, 83.5 percent disagreed or strongly disagreed. Just over one-quarter (26 percent) of the respondents held the position that they would first turn to the union for assistance.

63. DeMitchell and Cobb, *supra* note 43, 33.

64. "Unions protect, advocate for, and support professionalism according to these 71 respondents. The themes developed from the support professionalism prompt mirror the mean ($M = 3.63$) for "The union supports my ability to provide a professional service to my students" (Ibid. 34).

65. Ibid.

66. Ibid.

67. The concern about protection has been echoed by several commentators. For example, Terry Moe writes that "most people would be shocked" at collective bargaining agreements that "make it virtually impossible to dismiss teachers for poor performance." Terry M. Moe, "Union Power and the Education of Children," in Jane Hannaway and Andrew J. Rotherham. *Collective bargaining in education: Negotiating change in today's schools* (Cambridge, MA: Harvard Education Press, 2006): 237. And, "The burden of removing weak teachers has meant that principals often find it easier to shuffle poor teachers around the district than to remove them." Frederick M. Hess and Martin R. West, *A better bargain: Overhauling teacher*

collective bargaining for the 21st century (Cambridge, MA: Program on Education Policy & Governance, Harvard University, n.d.): 29.

68. Todd A. DeMitchell, "A reinvented union: A concern for teaching, not just teachers" in *Journal of Personnel Evaluation in Education* 11 (1998): 263.

69. DeMitchell and Cobb, *supra* note 43, 34–35.

70. Ibid. 35, comment from an elementary school teacher.

71. Ibid. 36, comment from a middle school teacher.

72. Ibid. 35, emphasis in original.

73. Ibid. 36.

74. Julia E. Koppich, "The as-yet-unfilled promise of reform bargaining: Forging a better match between the labor relations system we have and the education system we want," in Jane Hanaway and Andrew J. Rotherham (Eds.), *Collective bargaining in education: Negotiating change in today's schools* (Cambridge, MA: Harvard Education Press, 2006): 208.

75. DeMitchell and Cobb, *supra* note 2, 15. There is no significant difference between union leaders and non-union leaders on these statements.

76. Ibid.

77. DeMitchell and Cobb, *supra* note 43, 36.

78. DeMitchel and Cobb, *supra* note 2, 13. "A Bonferroni correction was made to the alpha level resulting in an adjusted significance level of .002" (10).

79. Ibid. 12.

80. DeMitchell and Cobb, *supra* note 43, 38.

81. Terry M. Moe, "Union power and the education of children," in Jane Hannaway and Andrew Rotherham (Eds.), *Collective bargaining in education: Negotiating change in today's schools* (Cambridge, MA: Harvard Education Press, 2006): 255.

82. Ronald D. Henderson, "Teacher unions: Continuity and change," in Ronald D. Henderson, Wayne J. Urban, and Paul Wolman (Eds.), *Teacher unions and education policy: Retrenchment or reform?* (Boston: Elsevier, 2004): 12–13.

Chapter 6

Reform and Labor Relations

> The collective bargaining process and resulting contract can either serve
> as one of the most effective vehicles for promoting and implementing
> educational reform or as a major obstacle to change.[1]

Larry Cuban asserts that education has a long history of reform.[2] In many
ways, although education is a conservative institution, it seems to always be
involved in reform. From the common school movement, to the progressive
movement, the rise of high schools and middles schools, the importation of
scientific management principles (Taylorism),[3] the crisis of Sputnick, and
the accountability movement of No Child Left Behind (NCLB) with its high
stakes testing, educators have been responding to change. Reform and collective bargaining are two potent forces that intersect and shape the landscape
of education.

In an era of reform, can unions and collective bargaining stand on the outside looking in? What roles do collective bargaining and unions play in an
era of reform? Hess and West writing about the education reform movement
in Massachusetts address this question, "Building on that start is no short
journey, but overhauling teacher collective bargaining is the critical next
step."[4] This chapter will review research that focused on school reform and
bargaining.

REFORM AND THE BARGAINING TABLE

Reform efforts must come to grips with collective bargaining. Any
educational change of lasting value must in some significant way be associated with the work of teachers. And, any changes in the terms and conditions

of employment must be bargained in school districts that have collective bargaining. What role does collective bargaining play when reform is on the bargaining table?

Myron Lieberman has argued that collective bargaining, regardless of other barriers, has stymied most reform efforts[5] and has held reform hostage.[6] However, the two major teacher unions have long held that the road to greater professionalism lies with a strong negotiated contract.[7] Regardless of whether collective bargaining is an impediment to reform or a vehicle for reform, both parties must "get it right" at the Table if reform is to be enacted.

"Collective bargaining and educational reform: for some these two terms fit together uncomfortably, for others they are a natural fit."[8] Unions were fashioned to secure wages, benefits, and terms and conditions of employment. How the NEA and the AFT become partners in educational reform is a challenge, especially if the reform is perceived as threatening the current order by realigning teacher rights and enhancing their responsibilities.

An example of the intersection of reform and bargaining is found in the implementation of No Child Left Behind federal legislation. "In school districts around the country, the Bush administration's centerpiece law on primary and secondary education is beginning to emerge as an issue at the bargaining table."[9] Teachers in Sandy, Oregon went on strike in part over the punitive aspects of NCLB—replacement, transfer and stringent new performance standards. In Philadelphia a union spokesperson stated, "At every turn in the contract negotiations, the press and demands of No Child Left Behind were always present."[10]

Reform, whether federal or state mandated or a local initiative must pass through the bargaining table in those school districts that collectively bargain. Given the large number of teachers covered by collective bargaining agreements, any reform initiative would have to gain at least grudging support from the unions in order to be successful. Unfortunately, the research on collective bargaining, unions, and reform is a "surprisingly small body of literature."[11] Judith Warren Little argues that there is scant knowledge about the "relative salience of the union compared with other sources in shaping teachers' response to or involvement in reform initiatives."[12] And, DeMitchell and Fossey posit that with "few exceptions, one will search in vain in the school reform literature for even the appearance of the word union."[13]

In sum, "[a] serious gap exists between what we think we know about teachers unions and what we really know."[14] The following fills in some of the gap about the relationship of reform and collective bargaining. Does educational reform have a favored place at the bargaining table? Or, is it just another opportunity to trade for something else of greater value—reform as a bargaining chip?

Unions and Reform

An early and important line of inquiry looked at the role of unions and reform. A RAND study of educational reform and bargaining found that union efforts to obtain status benefits such as increased participation in school-site decision making often engendered teacher suspicion, a feeling that the union was "falling down on the job" by not focusing on securing higher wages, better benefits, and more security.

The authors concluded that until "a union obtains these bread-and-butter items, a movement toward greater professionalism, is not likely."[15] Clearly, teachers expected their union to secure the material benefits of employment first; reform may be a distant second, or even worse, when teachers think of the role of their union. The job of the union is to protect the self-interests of its members and not to secure reform of education. Stated another way, the job of the union is to protect its membership not the students.

This finding is similar to Bascia's study that found that any union movement into new partnerships with administrators that enhance and expand teacher professionalism must be "logically consistent with teachers' historical needs for protection and representation."[16] Taken together, the RAND study and Bascia's research point to an expectation on the part of teachers, that their union must take care of their bread-and-butter issues of security, wages, and benefits.

If a union must take care of business first, when and under what conditions can it turn to issues of securing reform and greater professionalism given the fact that the union, like other interest groups, must compete for the district's scarce resources? Can collective bargaining and unionism, which were founded on self-interest, make the bridge to the reform goal of greater professionalism, which is based on service to another?

This question also takes on great import when viewed against a backdrop of the leadership of NEA's attempt to reinvent the union. Under the leadership of Bob Chase, the union tried to move from its traditionally narrow mission of protecting the interests of its membership to an expanded vision of professionalism that emphasizes that schools exist for children and not teachers and other employees "The NEA's movement toward a concern for teaching and not just teachers may cause its members to ask whether the union will still pursue the bread-and-butter agenda that typically induced them to join."[17] This challenge is discussed in Chapter 8.

Teacher, Union Representative, and the Principal

In another line of inquiry, DeMitchell and Barton conducted a five state study on the impact of collective bargaining at the school level because that is where reform is truly implemented if it is to mean anything.[18] At each individual school randomly selected for the study, they surveyed the principal, the school's union representative, and the first teacher listed alphabetically who was not the union representative. The study looked at what reforms had been undertaken by the school in the previous five years. It also examined, from the perspective of the three groups of respondents, the character and impact that collective bargaining had on their school's educational program.

The character of bargaining section of the research asked three questions. For all three groups, the more the collective bargaining process was viewed as problem solving the less the contract was considered an obstacle to reform. Similar results were found for the relationship between viewing the collective bargaining process as friendly and viewing it as an obstacle to reform. And, Bonferroni pair wise contrasts "showed that the union representatives viewed the negotiated contract as less an obstacle to reform than did the principals. Teachers' views were not significantly different from either of the two groups."[19] The teachers' view was neither closely aligned with nor significantly different from the other two groups—their union representatives and their principal, both of whom they work with daily.

The impact section asked two questions: "What impact did collective bargaining have on school reform efforts at your school?" and "What kind of impact has collective bargaining had on the quality of education that your school delivers to its students?" An ANOVA for the type of impact was significant with the union representatives viewing the impact as positive, principals viewing it as negative, and teachers, once again, were not significantly different from either group. A similar result was found for the impact of bargaining on the quality of education delivered by the school—union representatives positive, principals negative, and teachers not closely aligned with either group.

The authors concluded that bargaining has little impact on reform efforts at the school level as perceived by union representatives, principals, and teachers. The most surprising finding was two questions that the authors formulated after analyzing the data: "Do teachers care about bargaining and reform?" and "Whom do the union reps represent?"

DeMitchell and Barton expected that there would be disagreement between union representatives and principals on the impact of collective bargaining. They also expected to find that the teachers' views would be closely aligned with their union representatives because the union reps were not distant, bureaucratic functionaries; they worked in the same school as the responding teachers. What the researchers found was that as a group, teachers stood apart from their union representative's views. The teachers were more moderate than their representatives, and they were not "polarized along the same lines that polarize the management-union debate."[20] The lack of agreement between teachers and their union representatives on the centrality of collective bargaining to reform prompted DeMitchell and Barton to speculate whether "teachers just see collective bargaining as irrelevant to their classrooms."[21]

Bargaining Reform and the Superintendent

Another research article on bargaining and educational reform surveyed school superintendents and their perceptions of local school reform that was bargained. DeMitchell and Carroll surveyed superintendents from five different states representing five different geographical regions of the United States.[22] The superintendents were asked questions regarding the impact and ease of bargaining reform in their school district. The 88 respondents stated that a total of 149 reform initiatives were brought to the bargaining table. Of the 149 reforms brought to the bargaining table 24 (16 percent) were considered easy to bargain and 29 (19 percent) reforms were not successfully bargained. The mean for all reforms was 2.89 on a five-point Likert scale with one, "could not reach agreement" two, "moderately difficult," and five rated as "easy."[23]

Eighty-one percent of the reforms were successfully bargained and 19 percent were not. Small, rural school districts had the greatest difficulty in bargaining. The most difficult reform to bargain was extended day/year and the easiest reform was mentoring. Overall, the superintendents found it more difficult to bargain reform than it was easy to bargain reform. However, once a reform was bargained, superintendents perceived that there was some security attached to the reform. Thirty-six percent of the time school districts gave money unrelated to the reform in order to secure the reform initiative. Twenty-six percent of the time school districts gave up language in order to secure the reform.

In addition to the survey questions, the researchers asked an open-ended response question—did bargaining constrain or facilitate the bargaining of each reform. Fifteen percent responded in a positive manner that bargaining facilitated the implementation of the reform. For example, a suburban superintendent wrote "bargaining helped open the dialogue" on the proposed mentor teach program.[24] A superintendent from the northeast stated that bargaining "caused both sides to truly and deeply discuss the philosophy" on performance based pay.[25]

Forty-two percent of the 103 responding superintendent's comments were neutral. They were explanatory rather than taking a position of constrain or facilitation. Several wrote that bargaining reform in their district had "no impact" or "little impact."

The remainder of the superintendents, 43 percent characterized bargaining as a constraining force on the implementation of reform, more than double, almost triple, the number of superintendents who characterized bargaining as facilitating reform. . These comments were the most easily recognized because of the amount of frustration and anger that was expressed.[26] One superintendent from the southwest stated that collective bargaining" greatly constrained" the implementation of a new evaluation system. Another from the northwest wrote, "Those at the bargaining table lost sight of why schools exist."[27]

DeMitchell and Carroll conclude that educational reform is on the bargaining table but that it is not necessarily bargained with ease or with a strong sense of security that the reform will not be traded away in the future. Reform may have trouble with the rigorous give and take of the bargaining table. It appears that reform does not occupy a favored place at the table, and that it may become a bargaining chip "up for grabs during later rounds of bargaining."[28]

The last research on reform that will be discussed is unpublished. It focuses on the implementation of peer assistance and review in California.

Peer Assistance and Review

As part of its commitment to reform public education, California enacted a peer and assistance review program in 2001. Assembly Bill 1X established the California Peer Assistance and Review (PAR) Program for teachers.[29] This program was developed to assist teachers whose evaluations were not satisfactory. Assistance and support are provided by exemplary teachers and includes subject matter knowledge, teaching strategies, or both. This legislation was designed to allow exemplary teachers to assist veteran teachers and in the case of an unsatisfactory performance rating, participation is mandatory. It was instituted statewide, "at a time when no major district had implemented it in over a decade."[30]

The program replaced several professional development initiatives such as the Mentor Teacher Program that had been in existence for a number of years. While participation in the new initiative was voluntary on the part of the school districts, the loss of professional development monies and the requirement to report annually to the State Board of Education regarding the rationale for non-participation combined to provide a compelling reason for participation. The long and the short of it is that California's Peer Assistance and Review Program (PAR) is a state mandated school reform.

Peer assistance review is not to be confused with mentoring programs. PAR is more than just a buddy system. It was meant to have teeth. While PAR can and does use elements of coaching and non-evaluative support, it has the additional element of evaluation, which sets it apart from mentoring.

Kerchner and Koppich write that PAR is a "radical departure from established industrial norms" by "enforcing standards in their own occupation," thereby balancing the protection individual teachers with the protection of teaching."[31] The United Teachers of Los Angeles addressed this conundrum of unit members evaluating unit members on its website. The union wrote, "Every member's due process rights will still be protected by the union, but the union is assuming a deeper responsibility for helping struggling teachers improve."[32] The formal authority of teachers was increased by PAR by including them in the organizational structure of evaluation—a prototypical management function.

History and Research of PAR

The first bargained system of peer assistance and review occurred in Toledo, Ohio in 1981. Yet, it has only expanded modestly to approximately a score of school districts nationwide prior to the California legislation. The very low number of school districts that have adopted this strategy raises questions regarding the perceived efficacy of this reform. Yet, peer assistance review surfaced as a legislated reform strategy in California. The "solution" of using PAR to improve teacher quality has been around for 20 years, but has failed, until recently, to attach to a problem and be codified by politics to become policy.[33]

The majority of school districts and local teacher unions implementing PAR programs have the AFT as the exclusive representative of teachers. The American Federation of Teachers has a strong policy statement of support for PAR while the NEA has been ambivalent to lukewarm towards PAR. Since the NEA is the larger union, its ambivalence may have contributed to the near steady state in the number of PAR in school districts.[34]

Proponents of PAR assert "[p]eer review is probably the most powerful demonstration that teachers create and display knowledge of practice."[35] These most widely cited advocates for the benefits of peer assistance review use the subheading "Peer review brings higher standards to teaching."[36] In their book as an indication of the value they attach to the practice. With similar praise for PAR, Goldstein asserts that "PAR has proven more rigorous than traditional mechanisms for gate keeping of new teachers."[37] Adam Urbanksi speaking about the PAR program in the Rochester school system (New York) says, "It's an indispensable part of our drive to build the profession and contribute to better learning for students."[38] However, the Secretary of Education, Gary Hart, of Education for California cautions, "PAR is no silver bullet or panacea. But we believe strongly that it can be an opportunity for a new partnership between teachers and administrators to strengthen the profession."[39]

Several issue partisans have touted the benefits of PAR but little systematic, empirical research has been undertaken that could provide a research base for peer assistance and review. This is despite the 20 plus years since the implementation of the first peer review program. Kerchner and Koppich noted that the sample size was too small to allow for broad statistical comparisons, but stated that "historical evidence" in three school districts "show that more probationary and experienced teachers were dismissed under peer review than under the previous system of administrative review."[40] Yet, they state with Joseph G. Weeres that "[w]hen teachers evaluate other teachers, they are always tough and thorough."[41] However, Lieberman rebuts these conclusions characterizing the research on peer assistance and review as largely testimonials and not empirical research.[42]

However, Kerchner, Koppich, and Weeres cited a data set from the Toledo PAR program as support for the efficacy of the program. Kerchner, et al. wrote,

In the years that the Toledo internship program has been operating, approximately 6.4 percent of the new teachers resigned, were no renewed, or were terminated for inadequate performance. In the five years before the internship program began, when evaluation was done by administrators, only one new teacher was terminated.[43]

This single data set to support PAR is rather thin First, Kerchner constructed three categories for the internship (resignation, non-renewal, and termination) and compares them to one category for administrators (termination). How many, if any, new teachers resigned or were non-renewed when administrators were conducting the evaluations? Are all of the resignations and non-renewals only attributable to the PAR program? There is no data on what would have happened in the absence of the PAR program. Regarding the efficacy of PAR, Lieberman argued,

The new teachers of Toledo comprise about 7 percent of the district's total teaching force. Assume that nonrenewals under peer review differ from conventional review processes by 10 percent of the new hires. On an annual basis, peer review in Toledo would result in less than 1 percent difference in the district's teaching force. Obviously, the district staff would be overwhelmingly the same regardless of the presence or absence of peer review. Despite all the union promotion of peer review, it has very little potential for improving education.[44]

According to Bradley, 52 experienced teachers over 16 years were placed in intervention. There are 2,600 teachers in Toledo. If all 52 interventions took place in one year with the pool of 2,600 teachers, the interventions would account for 2 percent of the population of teachers. The average interventions of experienced teachers per year over the 16 years are 3.25 teachers placed in intervention out of 2,600 teachers. Some skeptics have pointed out the relatively small number of teachers who are "weeded out" under peer review.[45]

The Toledo experience, in addition to providing some data on PAR with conflicting conclusions, provides another backdrop for PAR as an educational reform initiative. Toledo's highly regarded peer-review program was canceled by the union in a dispute with the school board over extra pay for principals for extra work administering a new fourth grade proficiency test.[46] When the school board did not give into the union's demand to postpone the discussion with the principals until all of the employee contracts expired, the union made good on its threat to end the successful peer-review program. The teachers' union sacrificed a nationally acclaimed reform in order to pursue a union goal of "linked bargaining" with the district's nine bargaining unions. Commenting on the union's decision to unilaterally cancel this reform, Dal Lawrence, the union president, stated, "We don't take any great pleasure or pride in where we're at right now. This is an enormous price to pay."[47]

Reform was used as a bargaining chip to gain a union goal unrelated to quality education. A union goal trumped a reform that it sought and heralded as important thus questioning the security of a bargained reform. The Toledo experience of trading reform for union goals may dampen enthusiasm for the proposition that the collective bargaining table provides a useful forum for reform discussion.

The union also fought a proposal by the district administration to institute regular evaluations of tenured teachers. "Instead, principals can refer teachers for a performance review and assistance if they feel it is necessary, subject to the approval of the board of review that governs the program."[48] A skeptic may be moved to ask if the number of experienced teachers over 16 years has only amounted to 52 being placed in intervention, why would the Toledo Teachers Union want to limit the number of referrals if the goal is placing a caring, competent teacher in every classroom?

In a last research study on PAR, Goldstein conducted an embedded single-case design to study one urban school district. The study was conducted over a year and a half using observations, interviews, and surveys. The study focused on the distributed role of leadership, task division and task sharing. An interesting finding from the study was that while the cooperating teachers in the study recommended non-renewal in "unprecedented numbers" they were reluctant to be held "singularly responsible for the decisions that they had in effect made."[49] The Goldstein study raises the issue of whether teachers are ready to take on the responsibility of their professional decisions.

It is easy to make tough decisions for someone else to implement and to not take responsibility for the decision. Principals, typically, do not have that luxury.

If a goal of PAR is to use the practical and expert experience of teachers to make important decisions about who should teach, does the Goldstein study raise a concern whether teachers are willing to make the hard, public decisions necessary to protect teaching and not just teachers? Principals, who are given this charge, seem to have enough difficulty in this area. Will PAR overcome this proclivity to avoid the difficult but necessary decision?

Research on Bargaining California's PAR

As stated above, DeMitchell and Carroll conducted an unpublished study of the bargaining of PAR.[50] They started with an overarching question: Can the bargaining table in education, borrowed from the industrial union, meet the challenges of a complex delivery of professional services that relies heavily on context for application of knowledge as opposed to the rigid prescription often associated with a bargained contract? Is the industrial union bargaining table up to the challenges associated with the implementation of reform to support the delivery of professional services?

The purpose of this exploratory research was to examine the perceptions of California school superintendents and union presidents on the bargaining of peer assistance review programs in their respective school districts. In order to get a geographical spread two school districts in each of the 52 counties that had at least two school districts were randomly selected for inclusion in the study. The first selection of school district within a county was alternated between superintendent and union president. Once a school district was selected for either a superintendent's response or the union president's response, that school district was withdrawn from the pool. This decision was made so that the respondent would not have to take into consideration how her or his counterpart in the district was responding. The total number of potential respondents for the sample was 102.

Demographics

A total of 59 (58 percent) responses were received. Twenty-seven (44 percent of the total returned) were returned by association presidents and 35 (56 percent of total returned) superintendents responded

While it was clear that PAR was a state educational reform proposal, 52 percent of the responding school district including bargaining of PAR with other issues. Just over one-half of the California school districts lumped PAR

Table 1

Sessions:	1	2–3	4–5	6–7	8–9	10+	Total
# of School Districts	1	10	17	8	7	2	45
Percentage	2.2	22.2	37.8	17.8	15.6	4.4	100

with other labor issues. This raises the issue of whether reform had a favored place at the bargaining table for just other one-half of the responding school districts. There was no significant difference in outcomes regarding the level of the school district (elementary, high school or unified) or the location of the school district (rural, suburban, or urban).

Bargaining PAR took time even though it could be argued that it was a professional win for both parties—the assistance of educators to improve the quality of instruction delivered to students. The number of bargaining sessions over PAR is found below in Table 1. It took between two and five sessions for 60 percent of the bargaining sessions to reach a successful conclusion. What is unknown is why it took six, and over ten plus bargaining sessions (just over one-third of the responding school districts) to reach agreement when PAR would appear to benefit the profession of teaching and would provide a professional opportunity for teachers to police their own profession.

The number of bargaining sessions may be a window on the difficulty of the bargaining. When asked to characterize the bargaining of PAR (1= very easy to 5= very difficult) the mean for association presidents is 2.46 and for superintendents 2.52. The difference between the two means is not statistically significant. Overall, the association presidents and the superintendents found bargaining PAR to easier than difficult. When asked whether the respondents had fashioned a good agreement (1=strongly agree and 5= strongly disagree) that can be supported in the future, both association presidents (M=1.95) and superintendents (M=1.73) agreed.

However, when asked whether the bargaining table is a good forum for discussing reform issues, association presidents and superintendents differed significantly in their responses (*p*=.005). Association presidents had a mean of 2.33 (1= strongly agree and 5= strongly disagree) while superintendents had a mean on the other side of neutral of 3.39. Clearly, association presidents viewed the power of the table in dealing with reform issues more favorably than superintendents. This is a finding worth exploring in greater depth to ascertain its generalizibility to other reforms.

While the number of bargaining sessions may raise some questions, 73 percent of the school districts reported that the bargaining of PAR did not result in trade-offs for non-related issues. In other words, it appears that the extended bargaining sessions were not consistently the result of trade offs for money or language in order to secure the funding and implementation of PAR. Of the 27 percent of school districts that made a trade for PAR, 14 percent of them traded money unrelated to PAR, eight percent traded language, while five percent made other concessions unrelated to the implementation of PAR. Only 21 percent of the responding association presidents and superintendents thought that bargaining PAR was difficult or very difficult, while just under 46 percent believed that it was very easy to easy to bargain. A full one-third were neutral.

There is a last important finding from this exploratory research that helps to address the question about whether reform survives the bargaining table. Eighty-one percent of the respondents reported discussing professional issues (evaluation, instructional practices, staff development, and curriculum) at the bargaining table. It appears that bargaining PAR did not result to a large degree in using the reform practice in horse trading at the table. It may have provided an opportunity to discuss often-important educational issues.

While there was some trade offs for language and money, the extent of this trading is less than reported in the earlier DeMitchell and Carroll study. The first study found that money was traded for reform 36 percent of the time while the bargaining over PAR traded money for the reform 14 percent of the time. The earlier study traded language 26 percent of the time, while the PAR bargaining showed eight percent of the time language was traded. Was this outcome the result of the nature of the state legislation that offered an inducement to bargain an acceptable language, or is it an indication of a more professional approach in one state to bargaining that places professional interests equal with or above self-interests? I think that it is more likely that the special nature of this reform produced different results. PAR was tied to state legislation and failure to bargain would result in a net loss of funds to support teachers.

CONCLUSION

These studies raise the issue of whether reform has a favored place at the bargaining table. DeMitchell and Carroll's 1999 study found a moderate correlation at the .05 level (r=.387) that the more difficult the bargaining a reform the less secure the reform.[51] Conley, Muncey, and Gould in their interesting case study of bargaining new compensation systems[52] note the need for changes in bargaining to accommodate reform.[53] Can the bargaining table in education, borrowed from the industrial union, meet the challenges of a complex delivery of professional services that relies heavily on context for application of knowledge as opposed to the rigid prescription often associated with a bargained standardized contract? Is the industrial union bargaining table up to the challenges associated with the implementation of reform to support the delivery of professional services? Over 20 years ago Susan Moore Johnson posed the question, "Can schools be reformed at the bargaining table?"[54]

This question is important. Collective bargaining provides stability and consistency in work settings. It works best when the labor is easily standardized. But the reality of the classroom may not fit neatly into this formal structure of conditions of employment. It may provide some of the "what" of teaching but it is inadequate for the "how" of teaching. DeMitchell and Cobb's research on professionalism and unionism, discussed in Chapter 5, point to the limits of collective bargaining enhancing professional practice. Johnson, similarly, raises the question of whether collegial responsibility and pedagogical technique can be bargained well.[55]

However, this research does show that bargaining a reform can occasion a different approach at the table when both parties perceive a mutual gain and a potential mutual loss. Real educational reform is difficult to implement in the best of times. Educational reform must pass through the rigors of a collective bargaining table in which tradeoffs are commonplace. A reform changes practices and for many, change is loss. It is possible that the bargaining table is used as a brake on change, a way to say no or a way to say go slow within the guise of protecting interests unrelated to the reform being sought. It is also possible that the administration has not done a good enough job of selling the need for the reform. And it is also just as likely that the bargaining table assumes that all items are to be traded and *quid pro quo* must be served.

Whatever the explanations, both unions and administrators will likely have to find a way to separate bargaining over wages, benefits, and terms and conditions of employment from activities that pursue the public good of providing a quality service to the public. This does not mean that reform automatically trumps legitimate concerns found under the umbrella of negotiated contracts. It may mean that we need to do two things.

- First, develop a description of terms and conditions of employment that separate the conditions under which work is performed and the conditions under which a professional service is rendered.
- Second, as the DeMitchell and Barton study found, when bargaining is perceived as problem solving and is more friendly than hostile the less the contract was perceived as an obstacle to reform.[56] Administration should ensure that the reforms that they bring to the table are ones that are perceived as solving real problems in the school district and not just a shiny new bandwagon to jump on. Groundwork for the reform should be

carefully prepared with lots of opportunity for interaction at the informal level, the problem identification level, and the problem resolution level.

Schools and their educators must continue to use research into best practices and the data they gather in the schools to continual improve instruction. Reforms that impact the work of teachers must be bargained. Formulating and implementing reform is hard enough as it is, can we afford to place obstacles in the way of reform? Does the bargaining table and reform focus the tension between the roles of professional and union member? If yes, we should seek alternatives to allow pursuit of real reform inform the work of educators and to reduce the schism of us and them, management and union.

"We got the duty-free lunch," [Linda Bacon, president of the Pinellas Classroom Teachers Association] said of early union struggles. "Now we need to move to the really tough stuff—what we need to do as a union to drive student achievement."[57]

NOTES

1. For an interesting review of the literature on unionism and educational quality, see Charles Taylor Kerchner, *The relationship between teacher unionism and educational quality: A literature review* (National Education Association, November 2004). Site visited December 30, 2008 at http://209.216.233.244/kerchner/uploadImages/Kerchner-TUEQ%20Review.pdf.
"These studies, however, provide very little guidance to teachers, unionists, school administrators, or active citizens about how to conduct labor relations: what to bargain for, what to fight for, what to forge coalitions about" (38).
Lorraine M. McDonnell and Anthony Pascal, *Teacher unions and educational reform* (Santa Monica, CA: RAND, April 1988): X.
2. Larry Cuban, "Reforming again, again, and again" in *Educational Researcher* 19 (199) 3–13.
3. For an excellent discussion of Frederick Taylor and his scientific management theory as applied to education, see Raymond E. Callahan, *Education and the cult of efficiency* (Chicago: University of Chicago Press, 1962). George H. Martin, secretary of the Board of Education in Massachusetts, told his audience at NEA annual meeting in 1905, "the contrast between modern business methods and the most modern methods in education is so great as to suggest some searching questions. In the comparison, educational processes seem unscientific, crude, and wasteful" (Ibid. 6).
4. Frederick M. Hess and Martin R. West, "Taking on the teachers unions" in the *Boston Globe* (March 29, 2006): A11.
5. Myron Lieberman, "Educational reform and teacher bargaining" in *Government Union Review* 5 (1983): 54–75.

6. Myron Lieberman, *The teacher unions: How the NEA and AFT sabotage reform and hold students, parents, teachers, and taxpayers hostage to bureaucracy* (New York: Free Press, 1997).

7. Charles T. Kerchner and Julia E. Koppich (Eds.), *A union of professionals: Labor relations and educational reform* (New York: Teachers College Press, 1993).

8. Todd A. DeMitchell and Thomas Carroll, "Educational reform on the bargaining table: Impact, security, and tradeoffs." *Education Law Reporter* 134 (1999): 675. In their study, a superintendent from a small, rural school district in the south wrote, "Collective bargaining is a cancer on the educational process" (687).

9. Julia Silverman, "No child law irks teachers' unions," in the *Boston Globe* (November 13, 2005): A16.

10. Ibid.

11. Tom Loveless (Ed.), *Conflicting missions? Teachers unions and educational reform* (Washington, DC: Brookings Institution Press, 2000): 1.

12. Judith Warren Little, "Teachers' professional development in a climate of educational reform," in *Educational Evaluation and Policy Analysis* 15 (1993): 146.

13. Todd A. DeMitchell and Richard Fossey, *The limits of law-based school reform: Vain hopes and false promises* (Lancaster, PA: Technomic Publishing Company, Inc., 1997): 191.

14. Loveless, *supra* note 11, 2.

15. McDonnell and Pascal, *supra* note 1, 53. "Resocializing membership expectations is a task that must be accomplished before state and local teacher organizations can move toward active reform leadership in the outside environment" (53–54).

16. Nina Bascia, *Unions in teachers' professional lives: Social, intellectual, and practical concerns* (New York: Teachers College Press, 1994): 98.

17. Todd A. DeMitchell, "A reinvented union: A concern for teaching not just teachers," in *The Journal of Personnel Evaluation in Education* 11 (1998): 266.

18. Todd A. DeMitchell and Richard M. Barton, "Collective bargaining and its impact on local educational reform efforts," in *Educational Policy* 10 (1996): 366–78.

19. Ibid. 372.

20. Ibid. 377.

21. Ibid.

22. DeMitchell and Carroll, *supra* note 8.

23. Ibid. 682.

24. Ibid. 686.

25. Ibid. 687.

26. Ibid.

27. Ibid. 688.

28. Ibid. 691.

29. Chapter 4, Statutes of 1999 and *Education Code* Section 44505.

30. Jennifer Goldstein, "Making sense of distributed leadership: The case of peer assistance review," in *Educational Evaluation and Policy Analysis* 26 (2004): 173.

31. Charles Taylor Kerchner and Julia E. Koppich, "Organizing around quality: Examples and policy options from the frontiers of teacher unionism." *Organizing around quality: The policy implications of linking teacher unions and educational reform* (2003). Site visited February 9, 2004, at http://63.197.216.234/crcl/mindworkers/udpages/fulldoc.htm.

32. United Teachers of Los Angeles, "What is peer assistance and review?" Site visited December 30, 2008, at http://www.utla.net/par.

33. John W. Kingdon, *Agendas, alternatives, and public policies* (Glenview, IL: Scott, Foresman and Company, 1984) provides a model for understanding how an idea's time has come thus propelling it onto the public agenda for discussion and resolution. He posited that three "streams" or processes are linked as a way of gaining a place on the public agenda. The three streams are problems, policies, and politics. He argued persuasively that problem identification is not the only stream that runs through policy making, nor is it necessarily the beginning point for policy initiation. All three of these streams run separately but become coupled at critical points or "windows of opportunity." Kingdon wrote, "The probability of an item rising on the decision agenda is dramatically increased if all three streams—problems, policies, and politics—are joined" (187). The mixing of these multiple streams is not necessarily consistent with the model of rational decision-making. In fact, policy makers do not exclusively define the problem and then search for the one best solution. "More often, solutions search for problems" (91). Solutions and problems are both dumped into the "garbage can" as they are formulated. It is counterintuitive, but solutions are not always the outgrowth or response to a specific problem. Solutions exist independent of problems.

34. The National Education Association did not encourage peer assistance and review prior to 1997. The NEA Resolution D-8 adopted in July of 1997 is rather lukewarm towards PAR as compared to the AFT resolution. The NEA resolution states "[s]ome local associations may conclude that, under certain circumstances, a peer assistance or a peer assistance and review program is an appropriate mechanism" for improving professional practice (American Federation of Teachers, 1998, A7).

35. Charles Taylor Kerchner, Julia E. Koppich, and Joseph G. Weeres, *Taking charge of quality: How teachers and unions can revitalize schools. An introduction and companion to united mind workers* (San Francisco: Jossey-Bass Publishers, 1998): 32.

36. Ibid. 33.

37. Goldstein, *supra* note 30, 175.

38. Office of the Secretary of Education, *Peer assistance and review: Working models across the country.* (Sacramento, CA: California State University Institute for Education Reform, March 2000): 14.

39. Ibid. 7.

40. Kerchner and Koppich, *supra* note 31, at 2.

41. Charles Taylor Kerchner, Julia E. Koppich, and Joseph G. Weeres, *Taking charge of quality. How teachers and unions can revitalize schools* (San Francisco: Jossey-Bass Publishers, 1998): 33.

42. Myron Lieberman, *Teachers evaluating teachers: Peer review and the new unionism* (New Brunswick: Transaction Publishers, 1998): 91. See, also, Elizabeth E. Walen and Mimi DeRose, "New roles, new relationships: The power of peer appraisals," in *Educational Leadership* (1993). Site visited October 17, 2000, www.ascd .org/readingroom/edlead/9310/walen.

43. American Federation of Teachers, *Peer assistance and peer review: An AFT/ NEA handbook (draft)* (1998). Site visited February 27, 2001, at http://www.aft. org/edissues/paper, 0.

44. Lieberman, *supra* note 42, 93.

45. Ann Bradley, "Peer review programs catch hold as unions, districts work together," in *Education Week* (June 3, 1998): 1, 12.

46. Ann Bradley, "Toledo union eliminates peer-review program." *Education Week* (May 3, 1995) 3.

47. Ibid. 3.

48. Bradley, *supra* note 45, 12.

49. Goldstein, *supra* note 30, 191.

50. Todd A. DeMitchell and Thomas Carroll, "Bargaining peer assistance review in California: Reform on the bargaining table (unpublished research, n.d.). My friend and research partner died before we could finish the manuscript. I use this venue to place our research into the discussion on unions and collective bargaining. I miss him greatly.

51. DeMitchell and Carroll, *supra* note 8, 685.

52. For a short discussion of teacher compensation plans, see James H. Stronge, "Teacher compensation plan: An overview of options and issues," paper submitted to Hanover Public Schools, Hanover, NH (May 17, 2007). Site last visited December 31, 2008 at http://www.sau70.org/spotlight/TeacherCompen.pdf

53. Sharon Conley, Donna E. Muncey, and Jewell Gould, "Negotiating teacher compensation: Three views of comprehensive reform," in *Education Policy* 16 (2002): 675–706.

54. Susan Moore Johnson, "Can schools be reformed at the bargaining table?" *Teachers College Record* 89 (1987): 269–80.

55. Ibid.

56. DeMitchell and Barton, *supra* note 18.

57. Ann Bradley, "Fate of peer review rests with NEA locals," in *Education Week* (August 6, 1997): 14.

Section III

Practices

Chapter 7

Preparation and Practice: At the Table

Though they have attracted little media or, until recently, scholarly attention, teacher collective bargaining agreements shape nearly everything public schools do.[1]

It is the classroom that is the building block of the school, and it is the classroom that is central to student learning. Therefore, the classroom teacher stands at this crossroads of education. Little of lasting value can get done except through the efforts of teachers. Because the work of teachers involves terms and conditions of employment, a trigger for collective bargaining, what is bargained and how it is bargained is important.

Effectively bargaining a contract is hard work. To be successful requires organization, the ability to balance a number of issues at once and know how they interact with each other, to maintain a vision of your interests, and have the capacity to be tough, smart, understanding, honest, cognizant that you do not represent yourself at the table, and do it all while maintaining your integrity. There are no shortcuts to effective bargaining.

GOOD FAITH BARGAINING PRACTICES

Collective bargaining does not require that either side acquiesce to the demands of the other or that the two sides try to meet in the middle. The legal requirement, consistently found in both public sector and private sector collective bargaining is that each side bargain in good faith. The requirement to bargain in faith is the cornerstone of collective bargaining, public or private. But what is good faith?

There is a mutual obligation on the part of management and labor to bargain in good faith. Typically, the law requires both management and labor to meet at reasonable times and to confer in good faith with respect to wages, hours, and other terms and conditions of employment. This obligation does not compel either party to agree to a proposal or require them to make a concession. Both sides coming to the table as equals is a good beginning point for good faith. The practical rules for bargaining in good faith are:

- Approach bargaining with a mind accessible to persuasion.
- Follow procedures that will enhance the prospects of a negotiated settlement.
- Be willing to discuss freely and fully your respective claims and demands. When such claims and demands are opposed by the other side, be prepared to justify your claims with reason.
- Explore with an open mind proposals for compromise or other possible solutions of differences. Make an effort to find a mutually satisfactory basis for agreement.

The purpose of collective bargaining is to "bring to the bargaining table parties willing to present their proposals and articulate supporting reasons, to listen to weigh the proposals and reasons of the other party, and to search for some common ground which can serve as the basis for a written bilateral agreement."[2] The requirement to bargain in good faith is found consistently in state collective bargaining law[3] as well as in the National Labor Relations Board Act. Consequently, the failure to bargain in good faith is an unfair labor practice—a violation of the law (see Chapter 4 for a discussion of unfair labor practices).

Violations of good faith bargaining typically fall into one of two categories: per se and totality of conduct. A per se violation involves conduct on the part of one party that establishes a prima facie case of bad faith. It is conduct that is considered proof that the party's objective was to evade its duty to bargain in good faith. Per se violations include:

- Refusal to bargain.
- Delaying or conditioning bargaining
- Insistence to impasse upon a permissive subject of bargaining constitutes, regardless of justification, and a refusal to confer about mandatory subjects of bargaining
- Interference with a party's selection of bargaining team members
- By-passing a bargaining team's selected negotiators
- Refusal to discuss economic matters until agreement on all non-economic matters has been reached

- Refusal to execute a written agreement embodying terms which the parties had reached agreement
- Repudiation of a signed tentative agreement
- Refusal to provide pertinent information
  - This applies to bargaining as well as the processing of grievances because the union has the duty to represent unit employees. The information may be important in carrying out the duty to represent.
  - A request for information that involves wages and benefits carries a heavy presumption of relevance.
  - Union requests that fall outside of the ambit of wages and benefits, the union carries the burden of demonstrating pertinence.
  - There is no obligation that the requested material must be presented in any form that the union requests.
  - The employer only has to provide information that it actually has in its possession. It does not have to research or access other data bases in order to provide the information that the union wants.
- A unilateral change in wages or working conditions presently under negotiation.

The "totality of conduct" test looks to the entire course of negotiations to determine the party's subjective intent. It is the essence of surface bargaining that a party goes through the motions of negotiations, but in fact is weaving otherwise unobjectionable conduct into an entangling fabric meant to delay or prevent agreement.

The following are some factors that have been found to be indicative of bad faith bargaining under the totality of conduct test:

- Frequent turnover in negotiators.
- Negotiator's lack of authority which delays or thwarts the bargaining process.
- Lack of preparation for bargaining sessions.
- Missing, delaying, or canceling bargaining sessions.
- Insistence on ground rules before negotiating substantive issues.
- Taking an inflexible position.
- Regressive bargaining proposals.
- Predictably unacceptable counterproposals.

As stated above, but worth stating again, good faith bargaining does not compel either side to meet the other part way. It does not require that concessions be made; the difference between the sides does no have to split so that they meet in the middle. Making a concession may not serve the interests of a party. Hard bargaining in which one sides says "no" does not equate to bad faith. At times "no" can be the better, the more appropriate response. Good faith does require that both sides bring to the table a mind accessible to persuasion.

> Mahatma Ghandi—A "no" uttered from the deepest conviction is better than a greater "yes" merely uttered to please, or worse to avoid trouble.[4]

Closely read the language of the proposal. Listen carefully to the other side's reason for the proposal. What interests does it serve? Ask questions about the proposal to clear up ambiguities and inconsistencies. Ask questions that are designed to bring the proposal to your interests. If you find that the proposal is not in the best interests of the constituency who you represent at the table, say no.

For example, I was bargaining for a school district that had serious financial problems. The problem was compounded by the fact that the salary and benefits of the school district were considered to be a very high. The teachers had come to expect a good salary raise that would allow them to keep their relatively high position with neighboring school districts. With this backdrop I began negotiating a new contract. Every monetary item that came to the table resulted in me asking whether the net effect of this proposal would increase our long-term indebtedness or help us to solve the financial problem. We analyzed each proposal from the teachers union and from the classified employees union with this consideration in mind. We bargained hard but we approached each proposal in good faith to see if it would meet our interests or hinder our interests.

Only bargaining in good faith during negotiations is no substitute for a lack of good faith dealings during the year. As stated before the true measure of success of bargaining is not securing an agreement; success is when the relations between the parties improves, or at least does not deteriorate. Good faith should be a description of an ongoing process of good relations between educators.

Fisher and Ury in *Getting To Yes,* described in Chapter 4 offer advice that fits nicely with a discussion of good faith bargaining. They pose the following questions as a means of getting at acting in good faith:

- Is this an approach I would use with my good friends or family?
- Would I be embarrassed if a full account of my actions were printed in the local newspaper?
- If this were a book, would I be cast as the hero or villain?[5]

Good faith bargaining, hopefully leads to an "elegant" negotiation solution, a term used by David Kuechle, Professor Emeritus, Graduate School of

Education, Harvard University. Richard Fossey developed the following elegant solution:

1. The solution is better than any party's best alternative to a negotiated agreement.
2. All parties are committed to making the solution work.
3. The solution produces a good working relationship.
4. The solution is appropriate to long-term goals.
5. The solution can feasibly be implemented.
6. There is a clear understanding between the parties as to the meaning of the solution.
7. No joint interests are remaining to be addressed.
8. The process by which the agreement is achieved is seen by all parties as fair.[6]

THE BARGAINING TEAM AT THE BARGAINING TABLE(S)

There is no one best way to organize a bargaining team for bargaining at the table. I have not read research that points to "the best way," although it may exist. I offer my thoughts on how I have approached bargaining. The following is meant to spark a discussion and to raise questions, it is not meant as the definitive answer. It works for me but may not work for everyone.

I consulted with a school board bargaining team and the teachers' bargaining team one evening a couple of years ago. One of the best and feistiest discussions revolved around how I approached bargaining and the way in which I organized the team for table talk. This was one of the times during the evening in which the two teams found some agreement with each other. The important part of the conversation was that they talked to each other about what happens at the table and concluded that the way in which the teams organize for table talk is important and reflects an approach to bargaining.

I was the chief spokesperson for two school districts, once as the superintendent of a small rural school district and the other as the Director of Personnel and Labor Relations for a medium sized suburban school district, and offer the following for consideration and discussion.

• **You bargain with three groups**—your team, the other team, and your constituency, either the school board or the union's leadership council.

I found that some of my most difficult bargaining was with my team and the constituency whom I represented at the table. The bargaining with my team took place in caucus sessions when we reviewed our proposals and developed responses to the union's proposals. These discussions focused on strategies—what was working what was not working. I wanted these discussions to be open, unrestrained, and freewheeling. In the give and take of these negotiations on how to proceed, the team was at its best when it gave me its unvarnished opinion and questioned each other and me. Since I was responsible for negotiations I considered their comments, warnings, and suggestions and made the decision. I always let them know what was going to happen next. No surprises, is a good maxim.

Most often the constituency bargaining took place in closed session with the school board. You bargain with a school board over interests that are being served by bargaining including the impact of the monetary sections of the contract. Even though you are the professional and the expert on bargaining, the school board has the more powerful position as policy makers. That table was not the equal table shared with the union or the more lopsided table of bargaining with my team.

In this bargaining situation I used data and persuasiveness to steer the board in the direction that the superintendent thought was best. I tried to always be clear in these negotiations that we were discussing the substance of bargaining and not the strategy that would be used at the bargaining table. For those who have worked with school boards, they know the delicate dance over limits of board action that administrators do with school board members. I need to know my limits and the interests that I must pursue through these negotiations.

The third bargaining party is the other side. In my case it was the union. I have always represented management at the table. However, I have advised teachers and their unions about steps to take not only in bargaining but also in the broader labor relations of a school district.

- **The chief spokesperson does the talking at the table.** I ran a tight table believing that my bargaining team had ample opportunity to take part in the process during our caucus negotiations. I believe that one person representing a side can better control the flow of the conversation and keep it on track. Only one person at a time can drive the car, and as the chief spokesperson it is my responsibility to be the GPS system that keeps us moving in the right direction. The follow-up question is, if I am doing the talking, what is the rest of team doing?

I ask my team members to take notes during the negotiations (see below). When we receive a proposal from the other team, I ask my team to read it carefully and to ask any questions that they want so that we thoroughly understand the proposal, its possible impact, and to raise potential problems with the proposal. This takes place at the bargaining table. This is an important team action. The better we understand the proposal, its ramifications, and how it serves the other side's interests, the better the chance that we find if there is a community of interest that helps us to meet our interests as well.

A close reading of the proposal accompanied by questions seeking understanding of the proposal is a good communication strategy. Questions are also a good way to signal problems that you may have with the proposal in a less adversarial way. The give and take of questions and answers about a proposal can have a positive impact on table talk.

I do not assign members of the other team to each member of my team to watch. I believe that it is a waste of time to look for some signs that tell us what the other side is thinking. Our time can be better used in keeping accurate notes and participating in the discussion on the other sides' proposals. Listening to the other side and carefully reading their proposals tells us more about their intentions and interests than facial expressions.

This happens to be my way; it does not mean that it is the only way or even the best way. When I teach collective bargaining or when I am consulting with bargaining teams, I always point out that the team will need to find what works best for them. Some individuals like a more free flowing approach in which any member of the team talks when he or she wants to. However, the effectiveness of table talk should drive the decision and not the individual's need to talk.

- **The team needs broad representation**. I strive to have a representative from each school level on the bargaining team. Too often ideas that make sense at the bargaining table when discussing issues that need a resolution fail to meet the requirements of the real world of the school. I expect the principals or assistant principals on the team to keep the table talk grounded in the reality of the school where the contract is implemented and enforced.[7]
- **Keep the white horse in the stable and white knight at the round table**. Beware of the white knight on the white horse riding in to join the table talk with the solution that will result in a contract. There sometimes is the urge for someone with power who is not at the table to want to come in at the eleventh hour to "save" the contract by offering the solution. School board members, superintendents, and union presidents often want to mount up to save the day. While it may be satisfying for the individual, I have rarely found that it is effective in the long run. Once the knight has ridden up to the table, the dynamic shifts and the flow of negotiations changes. A potential backdoor to negotiations could possibly have been opened. The other team may believe that only having the knight at the table could get them what they want and consequently defer substantive discussions.

Bargaining is hard work. It involves building trust. If there is a perception that someone from outside the table can ride in, be it a school board member or a superintendent, the table will be in expectation of their arrival. Power shifts away from the table/team when the perceived real problem solver waits for entry to the room. I know that it is hard for leaders to stay away from the bargaining table, but they should either be at the table for the long haul or they should wait and fill their role by allowing the bargaining team to do its job.

PREPARING FOR BARGAINING

The mantra for preparing for bargaining is prepare, prepare, prepare. This is a lesson that I learned early, but I learned the hard way. Negotiations require data. Much of the data cannot wait until just before starting bargaining. Seniority lists, age of teachers for retirement purposes, history of comparator school district salary raises, fringe benefit costs, five-year comparison costs for early retirement packages, and grievance history are all data sources that the director of labor relations should consistently collect (The appendix has information on these and other topics for the Arroyo Wells School District Simulation). In addition to the grievance log that tracks the history of grievances, management and labor should each keep a bargaining book in which problems with the contract are recorded and labor relations issues that come up which could be addressed through the contract are also recorded.

In addition, when I was a school administrator our leadership team meetings always included a section on possible and pending grievances. This not only alerted the other school administrators about problems/issues they may soon face, but it had a centralizing effect. As the Director of Personnel and Labor Relations, I would often direct what the resolution should be for a pending grievance. This brought consistency to the enforcement of the contract and standardization of the contract. It also was a good communication tool in that the immediate supervisor would know if she/he would be supported in their response to the grievance at the next level.

For example, in one meeting an elementary school principal reported on a grievance that was just filed in her school. She told us what her preferred resolution was and why she wanted to deny the grievance. All of us discussed the grievance. I concluded the session telling her that I would have to accept the grievance and what the remedy would have to be and why. The decision was consistent with other similar grievances resolutions and the established practice. The principal stated that she believed that she had to follow her course of action to deny the grievance in order to send a specific message. We agreed that she could take that action knowing full well that I would not support her at Level Two of the grievance.

The next section discusses how scattergrams are used and their relationship to stream of earnings calculations in preparation for bargaining.

SCATTERGRAMS

In order to bargain salary, it is imperative that the school district know the distribution of employees on the salary schedule. This information is also necessary for the union to know as well. Without this knowledge it is very difficult for either side to discuss and trade proposals that are grounded on facts. A scattergram is a useful tool for organizing and displaying data on the distribution across the salary schedule. In addition, a school district can use scattergrams as historical data to help ascertain patterns in movement across the columns of the salary schedule. The salary schedule from the Arroyo Wells School District simulation found in Appendix A is used as an example of a scattergram. The salary schedule for the Arroyo Wells simulation is copied below and is used again in the Stream of Earning discussion that follows.

To develop a scattergram use the vertical column for years (step) and the horizontal columns for education/credits (column) without the actual salary. The same idea holds for the horizontal axis of earned graduate credits. List the number of teachers on each step and column point on the grid. The

Arroyo Wells School District Salary Schedule

Year	BA	BA+15	MA	MA+15	MA+30
1	34,121	35,266	38,343	41,740	44,520
2	34,529	36,466	40,064	43,183	46,195
3	36,119	38,688	41,909	45,171	48,292
4	37,784	40,467	43,822	47,252	50,519
5	39,513	42,328	45,851	49,424	52,836
6	41,332	44,266	48,004	51,745	55,318
7	43,292	46,363	50,324	54,243	57,985
8	45,273	48,487	52,868	57,084	61,029
9		50,646	55,508	59,554	63,351
10		52,870	59,058	63,584	66,945
11					69,545

Source: Education Stipend—Added to Base Salary—Cumulative
CAGS/CAS/Ed.S.= $1,000
Ed.D./Ph.D. = $2,500

Longevity Stipend—Added to Base Salary and Education Stipend—Non-Cumulative
12 to 13 years of continuous service in AWSD = $750
14 to 16 years of continuous service in AWSD = $1,500
17 to 19 years of continuous service in AWSD = $2,000
20 to 25 years of continuous service in AWSD = $2,500
26 + years of continuous service in AWSD = $3,000

Scattergram: Arroyo Wells School District

Year	BA	BA+15	MA	MA +15	MA+30	Total
1	1					1
2		2				2
3	1	1				2
4	1	1				2
5	1	1				2
6		3				3
7	2	2	2			6
8	*	1	1			2
9	*	5	5	5		15
10	*	25	22	15		62
11	*	*	*	*	78	78
Total	6	41	30	20	78	175

Source: B.A. = \$234,121

B.A.+15 = \$2,043,406
MA = \$1,730,332
MA+15 = \$1,251530
MA+30 = \$5,424,510
TOTAL Salary = \$10,683,899

Stipend for each degree held
CAGS—\$1,500 stipend added to salary each year X 18 = \$27,000
Ed.D/Ph.D.—\$2,500 stipend added to salary each year X 7 = \$17,500

Longevity Stipend—Added to Base Salary and Education Stipend—Non-Cumulative
12 to 13 years of continuous service in AWSD = \$750 X 14 = \$10,500
14 to 16 years of continuous service in AWSD = \$1,500 X 16 = \$24,000
17 to 19 years of continuous service in AWSD = \$2,000 X 17 = 34,000
20 to 25 years of continuous service in AWSD = \$2,500 X 27 = \$67,500
26 + years of continuous service in AWSD = \$3,000 X 69 = \$207,000
TOTAL Stipends = \$387,500

GRAND TOTAL FROM SALARY SCHEDULE = \$11,071,394

asterisk means that there are no placements possible for that intersection of year (step) and education (column). Below is the scattergram for the 175 teachers in the Arroyo Wells School District. It is also found in the Appendix A-10.

The scattergram not only gives the distribution of the faculty on the salary schedule, it also allows for additional data gathering by computing the cost of each column. Scattergram data over time provide information for budget planning such as how long does it typically take a person to move from one track to another. The template of the scattergram gives administration the ability to look at the relative costs between elementary, middle school, and high school faculties by developing a scattergram for each level. The template can also be used to disaggregate the data by individual schools.

This scattergram shows that there are a number of teachers (25) who have not been able to make the jump to the M.A. column. The M.A. requirement is possibly presenting an obstacle to column movement. The union may seek a change to the MA column to one that does not require the MA, such as BA+30/MA. Almost 82 percent of the faculty have 12 or more years of service in the district. This may result in pressure to increase the amount of the longevity stipend, or there may be a push for an additional year (step) on the salary schedule. With 78 teachers (44.6%) at the last column, there may be a push for another column, M+45 possibly.

This knowledge allows management to anticipate potential proposals to change the salary schedule, thus giving them time to ascertain if it serves the interests of the district to make a change. For example, adding post BA units to the MA column may be considered as diminishing an interest in having a faculty with a focused graduate program that a master's degree provides as opposed to a collection of possibly unconnected graduate credits.

The 20, 25, 30 Stream of Earnings Approach:
A Means for Comparing Salaries

The ability to compare salary schedules is important for preparing documentation on salary proposals. Linda Kaboolian discusses the benefit of salary benchmarking, a bargaining strategy that may fit well the stream of earnings approach discussed below. Salary benchmarking uses salary schedules from nearby school districts "to set the standard."[8] This is a two-step process. First, negotiate which school districts will serve as comparators. Second, decide how will the salary schedules be compared? Do the parties use the beginning salary step, the middle/median step and column, or the last step and column? Unfortunately, the process too often becomes an exercise in cherry picking with each side selecting the point on a salary schedule that supports their position as opposed to a search for some objective data.[9]

I prefer the stream of earnings approach mainly because it takes into account salary schedules that are front-loaded in order to attract candidates and end-loaded salary schedules designed to keep employees. It also provides for a way to account for differences in longevity stipends step differentials (maximum number of years on the salary schedule—12, 14, or 15 years), and graduate credit differentials (e.g., number of units needed for a track change and when a masters degree is required).

One way to address this problem of what to compare is to look at how much to compare, a single point or multiple points on the salary schedule. I suggest using the stream of earnings approach. The stream of earnings approach starts with a set of parameters that you apply consistently to the salary schedules being compared. Basically, you track the earnings of an employee who starts with a school district in his/her first year of employment and stays 20, 25, or 30 years. This approach helps to take into account variability of salary schedules. This approach will not describe what the salary schedule should look like. It will help the parties to see the relative fairness of the compared salary schedules.

Below is a sample parameter. These parameters will change to accurately reflect the pattern of the school district in which bargaining is taking place. The key is for the two sides to agree on the parameters ahead of time. District data on these parameters is very helpful and reduces arguments over what parameters exist in your school district.

Arroyo Wells School District Stream of Earnings

Year	Salary	Comments	Running Total
1	34,121		34,121
2	34,529		68,650
3	36,119		104,769
4	37,784		142,553
5	39,513		182,066
6	44,266	Column Movement (CM)	226,332
7	46,363		272,695
8	48,487		321,182
9	50,646		371,828
10	52,870		424,698
11	52,870		477,568
12	52,870	+ 750 longevity, 53,620	531,188
13	52,870	+ 750 longevity, 53,620	584,808
14	59,058	CM received MA +1,500, 60,558	645,366
15	59,058	+1,500 longevity, 60,558	705,924
16	59,058	+1,500, longevity, 60,558	766,482
17	59,058	+2,000, longevity,61,058	827,540
18	59,058	+2,000, longevity 61,058	888,598
19	63,584	CM +2,000 longevity, 65,584	954,182
20	63,584	+ 2,500, longevity, 66,084	1,020,266
21	63,584	+ 2,500, longevity, 66,084	1,086,350
22	63,584	+ 2,500, longevity, 66,084	1,152,434
23	63,584	+ 2,500, longevity, 66,084	1,218,518
24	66,945	CM + 2,500 longevity, 69,445	1,287,963
25	69,545	+ 2,500 longevity, 72,045	1,360,008
26	69,545	+ 3,000 longevity, 72,545	1,432,553
27	69,545	+ 3,000 longevity, 72,545	1,505,098
28	69,545	+ 3,000 longevity, 72,545	1,577,643
29	69,545	+ 3,000 longevity, 72,545	1,650,188
30	69,545	+ 3,000 longevity, 72,545	1,722,733

Sample Parameters

- The salary schedules selected for comparison do not change for purposes of the analysis. The idea is to keep it simple.
- Employee moves down for each year of service, which will be continual for 30 years.
- Every year the employee accumulates three (3) credits toward column movement on the salary schedule.
- The teacher receives a master's degree at the 14th year of employment.

The stream of earnings approach using the Arroyo Wells School District Simulation salary schedule is found above.

Start at step one, column one. The salary is $34,121. Keep a running total. For the second year the salary is $34,529 and the running total is $68,650. Move down for the third year to a salary of $36,119 and the total of salary over the three years is $104, 769. This same pattern is repeated for years four and five. For year six, the teacher has enough units to move over to the next column BA+15 (Column Movement/CM). The teacher is now making $44,266 (Year six and column BA+15). The running total for the teacher with six years of service is $226,332. The sample stream of earning below completes the 30 years of continuous service in the Arroyo Wells School District. However, comparisons can be made at any point during the 30 years of service. The years of service can also be extended beyond 30 years, but there may not be much of a return on this extra amount of work.

You can try the stream of earning using the Arroyo Wells School District parameters with the Metroville School District and the Happy Valley School District and compare the stream of earning at the 20 year, 25 year, and 30 year points. This method of salary comparisons can be used with most salary schedules to develop comparisons that are truly comparable and not just the product of cherry picking. Meaningful, reliable, and shared data facilitate negotiations.

PROPOSALS, SUPPOSALS, AND THE WATER COOLER

A proposal is a written document exchanged with the other party at the bargaining table. It is language intended to be used in the contract being bargained. It is the major way in which the parties at the bargaining table trade and discuss what they are seeking in the contract. Contract language contained in the proposal seeks clarity and transparency. A good rule of thumb is borrowed from substantive due process analysis; would the reasonable person know what to do or what not to do upon reading the language. Policy often works best with some ambiguity, some vagueness, some wiggle room; contract language does not. Contract language must be explicit, direct, clear, and use simple language.

When preparing a proposal it is not necessary to restate every section that currently exists in the contract for which you are not requesting a change. I, and others, have designated sections that are unchanged simply as "no change." This has the added benefit of directing attention to the changes in the current contract. The goal of proposals is to be clear about intentions and language. This is important as an overall strategy of improving labor relations. To hide the impact of language is to invite retaliation in the next round of negotiations and there is always another round of negotiations. Trust is built on openness; it is injured through deception.

The following is an example of a proposal using the Arroyo Wells School District Simulation. You will note that the upper left hand corner of the proposal has the date and time when the proposal was offered. It also designates that it is a management proposal and it states that it is management's second proposal on this contract section. This is important for keeping track of the proposals.

District #2

3/25/08
3:46 pm

Article 9
Class Size

9.1 General

The following class sizes shall be defined as applicable for all schools in the District:

Grades: K   25
Grades 1–3   26
Grades 4–5   27
Grades 6–12   30 with the exception of science laboratories which shall have a maximum of 24 students.

9.2 Combination Classes
The class size for elementary classes, which combine one or more grade levels shall be reduced by one. The lower class size shall be used as the base for the reduction in class size.

9.3 Preparation time for middle and high school—No Change

9.4 300 Minutes of Preparation time every ten work days—No Change

9.5   Student Class Assignments

Student class assignments shall be made by the principal, or his/her designee. If student class assignments have been made by that would go over the class size limits stated in 9.1, the principal, or designee, shall follow the procedures below:

9.51 No Change

9.52 No Change

9.53 If the foregoing approaches do not work to bring the class size into the prescribed limits stated above, the District may choose to implement the class size bonus plan below or hire a teacher to reduce the adversely affected class size.

    A. A teacher who exceeds the maximum class size for ten (10) consecutive days shall on the eleventh (11) consecutive day be paid ten (10) dollars per day per student over the maximum, retroactive back to the first day the class size maximum was exceeded. The District may end this practice in an individual classroom by reducing the class size to the prescribed maximum or less.

    B. There will be a period during the first three weeks of the semester in which 9.53 A will not be in effect so as to allow the District the ability to move students.

    C. The District shall place no more than two students over the class size limit in any one class.

    D. The class size stipend will not be calculated into the base salary and shall remain a bonus. The affected teacher shall be paid once a month for the class size bonus.

Teachers affected by this class size bonus shall complete all District generated paperwork in accordance with reasonable timelines.

If the proposal has been tentatively agreed (TA) to by both parties, I recommend that both parties sign each page of an original proposal. I always TA's the proposal with my signature at the end of the document with the date and I initial every page with the date. I also signed or initialed each page immediately below the last line of the page. My goal was to allow as little room as possible between the last line and my signature/initials.

Another type of proposal is a packaged proposal. This type of proposal ties one or more sections of the contract together. For example using the Arroyo Wells School District Simulation, a packaged proposal could include early retirement, salary, and grievance language. It is important that both sides realize that a package proposal is cut from whole cloth. It cannot be separated out with the other party stating that it will accept, for example, the grievance section but not the other parts and expect that the packaged proposal would bind the moving party. The packaged proposal is accepted as a package or not at all. I recommend to my class that packaged proposals work best towards the end of negotiations rather than at the beginning. It is important to package proposals so that both parties can see the relationship between the sections and the overall interests of the parties.

Technology at the Table

In my spring 2009, collective bargaining class, a labor team (I had two different bargaining tables using the Arroyo Wells School District simulation.) added a level of technology that was not available when I bargained and had not been used before in my other simulations. Their use of technology is worth considering as a tool for bargaining.

First, Labor Team B set up a wiki (http://collectivebargaining.wetpaint.com) for their team to share information and to develop proposals. Anyone on the team could post suggested language changes and the other team members could comment on the changes and offer their own. Danielle Bolduc, Director of Learning, Instruction, Research, and Technology stated, "The wiki always [allowed] everyone to comment and offer suggestions on their own time. It also allows a larger group to discuss the articles without one or two people dominating the conversation."[10] Danielle established the wiki. She believes that it facilitating their development of proposals.

Second, the labor team used an LCD projector for proposals. The labor team projected their proposals onto a screen in the bargaining room. Their proposal became the basis for discussion with management. Changes were made using the track change function and projected for both teams to see. The track change function helped to separate the labor and management changes. Labor controlled the LCD screen and used their proposal as the basis for the table talk.

The chief negotiator for the Labor Team B, Travis Nadeau a high school social studies teacher, stated that the use of the projector "became the base line for discussions with management. When management questioned a specific section of the proposal labor asked what changes they would suggest."[11] It kept the discussion of the proposal moving forward without the need for frequent caucuses. But, supposals had a tendency to be translated into proposals thus altering the free flow and exchange of ideas that may not yet be fully formed.

While the technology allowed for quick changes to proposals, an unintended consequence may be that it was more difficult for the team not controlling the projector to call a caucus. They would have to walk away from the table talk. But, the teams must do that so as to not be stampeded into a decision that was available through technology but was not necessarily in their constituency's best interest.

Speed and efficiency at the table may not always serve the interests of the constituency represented. Technology for technology sake is probably a false path.

There may be a need for a certain dance at the table in which table talk allows individual to gauge the response of the other side. The "what ifs" of supposals and questions should not fall prey to the immediacy of technology. I was struck at times how it was the projected word that captured attention and not the spoken word. With everyone facing the screen, often everyone talked to the screen and not to each other. As stated earlier in the book, labor relations in education are people intensive; we can use technology but we must not be captured by it. At the end of the day, or the end of the session, bargaining is talking to the other person and not just exchanging proposals.

Talking at the Table

The bargaining table is designed for talk. Therefore, the type of talk that takes place at the table is important. It helps to develop trust, defines the quality and interest in personal relations; it provides the place for the human element of collective bargaining. The two sides talk to each other, most times civilly but not always. Passion can run high because issues of power and worth lurk just below the surface of the discussion. The quality of the table talk—defined as the conversations that take place when representatives from both labor and management sit together at the bargaining table—and the quality of the proposals impact the outcome of bargaining.

Michael Jette studied the table talk at New Hampshire public school bargaining sessions for his dissertation at the University of New Hampshire. He found that both union leaders and school superintendents in his study believed that table talk impacted the outcome of bargaining. Almost 94 percent of the teacher union leaders and 91 percent of the management team leaders described their table talk as either extremely related or related to the outcome of bargaining.

One of the issues that he focused on was whether the table talk was primarily debate or dialogue, using Berman's construct of Public Conversations.[12] Adapting Berman's construct to the collective bargaining table, Jette posed some of the following debate/dialogue paired statements in which respondents were asked to choose their position along a continuum between the statements:

Debate "Our 'table talk' sought to find flaws and counter arguments."

Dialogue "Our 'table talk' sought to understand, find meaning and find agreement."

Debate "The 'table talk' put forward our best thinking, and defended it against challenge to show that it was right."

Dialogue "The 'table talk' put forth our best thinking, knowing that the reflections of others would only help to improve rather than to destroy it."[13]

Jette also found a moderate correlation *(p* = .320) for both labor and management between the dialogue/debate score and success of bargaining—the greater the dialogue, the greater the success and the greater the debate the lesser the success.[14] In addition, he found that respondents who reported their bargaining to be unsuccessful or highly unsuccessful tended to report that the table talk was "oppositional," "an attempt to prove the other side wrong," and the table talk was used to defend against challenge and to show their side was "right," the parties failed to listen to each other, and the people were belittled or offended.[15]

A supposal uses table talk; it is not a proposal in the traditional sense. A proposal is a formal statement, whereas a supposal is an invitation to explore options. It starts with "what if we. . . ." It allows the parties to brainstorm and explore without feeling that either side is constrained by the formality of a proposal. This is effective in breaking out of the rut of trading proposals with little to no discussion. This allows for bargaining to be the problem solving activity that DeMitchell and Barton found that the more bargaining was viewed as problem solving the less it was viewed as" an obstacle to reform."[16] It also can be an opportunity for dialogue as opposed to debate.

Water cooler negotiations is the last form of negotiations. Water cooler negotiations are informal conversations that take place away from the table between the chief negotiators of both parties. I have initiated these conversations by calling a caucus and then suggesting that my counterpart looked thirsty. This meant that I wanted to have a conversation away from the table. Water cooler negotiations can work when one of the two sides wants to "float" some idea that can break the stalemate that has occurred at the table. It is similar to a supposal except that it takes place away from the table and is between the chief negotiators, whereas supposals occur at the table with both teams. The danger of this strategy is that either bargaining team could believe that a private deal was being discussed that bypassed them.

This can be an effective strategy but it must be used sparingly. It provides an informal opportunity to explore options that may result in a formal proposal. It must also be used in such a way that your bargaining team does not lose its trust in the chief spokesperson.

Water cooler negotiations work best when the discussion at the water cooler is brought back to the respective teams for further discussion. From there, they can be brought to the table. To treat water cooler negotiations as the same as a proposal may harm the informality of this type of negotiations in the future. Water cooler negotiations can be a valuable strategy, but it should not be overused.

MANAGING INFORMATION

Bargaining often involves handling large amounts of information. How to manage that data in a meaningful way that facilitates bargaining is a challenge. I use a multi-faceted approach. I start with the proposition that managing the information is important; therefore I must construct a procedure that reflects that importance. Management of data helps to keep bargaining moving forward; it provides a basis for comparing proposals; it provides a record of intentions, and it provides a record for possible unfair labor practice charges and arbitration hearings. Another important reason for managing information is that a bargaining team never wants to counter its own proposal. Keeping track of which side presented a proposal last helps to avoid this cardinal bargaining sin. It is important but too often it is approached in a haphazard manner. I will briefly bullet my approach to managing information below.

Minutes

As I stated above, all members of the bargaining team take notes on each bargaining session. They try to capture the table talk, identify who was at the table, and track the approximate of the passage of time. I gather all of the notes from my team, adding my own notes. From those notes I write the official minutes. I share my draft with the team for accuracy. Once we have reached agreement, I destroy the working minutes and keep one set of official minutes. The one set for each bargaining session is then used for all subsequent negotiations and any subsequent legal proceedings. I strive for the greatest accuracy that I can get.

I keep a copy of the minutes for my bargaining binder and store the original with my signature and date in the bargaining file. One copy is used for current negotiations and the original is used for historical reference and future use. I do not underestimate the power of a written document. We write, including minutes, for three audiences—our side, the other side, and a neutral third party (arbitration, unfair labor practices, and/or a court proceeding. I do not distribute the minutes to the other side, but I will quote from them to make a point at the table.

Proposals

Proposals for specific contract sections are numbered and kept together. Similarly, packaged proposals are also kept together numerically. I keep a three-ring binder with each section of the contract tabbed. The first sheet is the existing contract language. Following the original I place in order each proposal. If the union proposal is not numbered, dated, and timed I will add those notations. This allows me to see the progression of bargaining on an individual section of the contract. By reviewing the packaged proposals I can make a notation for each individual contract section that it has been included in a package.

Tentative Agreements (TA)

I keep all originals of the tentative agreement in a file with the minutes in a locked fireproof file cabinet. I make a copy of the tentative agreements and the minutes in a second bargaining book which I bring to the table.

Overall Bargaining

At the front of my three-ring bargaining binder I keep a contract master list that lists each contract section vertically. Horizontally, I set up a series of columns with alternating titles of district and union. For each contract section I enter the number of the proposal for each side. When a section has been signed off as a tentative agreement, I write TA in capital letters.

This contract list is important for keeping track of where each section is in bargaining. I periodically review my list with the other team to make sure that we have agreement. There is nothing worse than one side believing that a contract has reached a tentative agreement and the other does not. It is prudent to check with the other side. If there is a disagreement I use the second bargaining book with a copy of the TA section and the minutes that recorded the TA.

PAST PRACTICE

Past practice is an often-stated concept but most often it is little understood. A past practice becomes important when the contract is silent on a particular practice. Consequently, a past practice is typically not written down. The key is that the past practice must be a consistent and clear practice and not an isolated event. The practice must have occurred over a period of time. It must be known and accepted by both parties. The party asserting a past practice typically carries the burden of demonstrating that the practice existed and under what conditions it has occurred. The Supreme Court of New Hampshire provides some useful guidance in this area.

In an appeal from a New Hampshire Public Employee Labor Relations Board (PELRB) decision (2007-026), the Tamworth Educational Support

Personnel Association alleged that the school district had agreed to a just cause provision through past practice and statements made in the collective bargaining negotiations. There was no specific provision for just-cause bargained into the contract language. On the issue of what constitutes a past practice, the Court wrote (some internal citations omitted):

> Under certain circumstances, custom and past practice may establish an implied term of a collective bargaining agreement. In *Appeal of New Hampshire Department of Safety,* for instance the evidence established that the past practice at issue existed "over the course of the employment relationship" between the union and the employer. The practice continued openly, was never modified by multiple collective bargaining agreements into which the parties entered, and inexorably led the PELRB to conclude that "both parties had knowledge that the past practice existed and by their respective actions over the protracted period of time demonstrated acceptance of it" By contrast, the evidence [in the *Appeal of Tamworth*] concerned a single employee's experience in July 2005. The PELRB reasonably determined that this offer of proof was insufficient to establish a binding past practice.[17]

CONCLUSION

Negotiating a good, sound contract is hard work. It takes patience, diligence, and organization. Problem solving skills, communication skills, the ability to look someone in the eye and say no and then provide a rationale for the position, and an ability to gain trust and to give trust when earned are important qualities.

A last piece of advice is to thoroughly analyze the existing contract language before bargaining new language. Very seldom is obsolete language deleted from a contract. New language for new concerns is just tacked on. I found language in a contract that talked about the fair use of the old hand cranked mimeograph machines; a machine that I used when I first started teaching fourth grade four decades ago. Contract sections should be reviewed looking for problems and highlighting deadlines. My students, as one of their assignments, are required to analyze a school district's contract language looking for the good, the bad, and the ugly. Reading contracts with a critical eye is important in bargaining a contract as well as managing a contract's implementation.

Not all contract sections are well written. A poorly written contract section can lead to problems of implementation and contract creep in which the contract continues to expand in directions that do not serve the interests of management. Preparation for bargaining should include a detailed review of all contract sections looking for ambiguity, poorly written language, contradictory language and vague language. These are a few of my good, bad, and ugly concerns about contract language.

- Too often contract language allows for "two bites of the apple" in which a legal right granted in state and federal law is stated as a right in the contract, thus allowing two opportunities to seek relief. If a right is granted by statute an inclusion of the right in the contract is superfluous. It gives the employee a grievable right unless there is positive assurance stating that the section is not grievable and thus not subject to arbitration. The legal remedy for the right should be the avenue used to seek redress of the right. William Sharp also agrees that it is not good management practice to agree to including statutes in the contract.[18]

In addition, I have found contract sections that allow employees to grieve alleged violations of board policy. As discussed previously, the grievance hat is a narrow hat in which only the contract fit under it. The grievance process should not be the general vehicle for all conflict resolution.

- Use positive assurance to bracket those sections that you do not want to be grieved or arbitrated. It is best to be very explicit when a contract section is not subject to the grievance process. For example, the following taken from a contract is a succinct statement giving positive assurance: "The transfer decision is not grievable." Clear language like this reduces the likelihood of misunderstanding and/or allowing an unintended consequence of grieving and arbitrating a topic not intended to be grieved or arbitrated.
- Bargaining an ongoing early retirement incentive into the contract requires management to offer more than it would have if it wants to target a specific time for an incentive. I believe that the early retirement incentives should only be bargained with a clear sunset provision that limits the time in which the incentive is offered. When I bargained an early retirement incentive the incentive was only available for one year and the proposal had to save money for the school district over a five-year period. I was always upfront about this requirement and that it was an incentive for retiring earlier than expected rather than a benefit of employment. A copy of how to do a five-year cost analysis when preparing an early retirement proposal is included in the simulation in Appendix A-5.

It is only advantageous to the school district to offer an incentive if it induces an employee to retire this year rather than waiting another year or two. The employee who was going to retire anyway gets a bonus, and the district has spent money with no additional return.

A second issue associated with ongoing retirement incentive plans, is that they are sometimes capped as to the number of individuals who can access the benefit. This underscores that the purpose of the section is a benefit and not an incentive. If early retirement is an incentive you place a minimum on who can access it but not a maximum number of teachers as long as the requirement that within five years the district will save money is met. Early retirement can be both a personnel incentive—making room for newer teachers—and a financial incentive—replacing higher paid teachers with lower paid teachers—for school districts.

- I have come across grievance language that goes from the informal to the formal with the immediate supervisor, step two with the superintendent, step three with the school board, and step four with the arbitrator who renders a binding decision compelling the school board to implement the decision. It seems to me that the school board should not be one of the steps in a binding arbitration process. Politically it places them in the position of having their position publicly overturned. The school board is placed in one of those rare situations in which their decision will ultimately be advisory to the next and final level of the decision process. Second, it adds time to the process. I would leave the school board out of the steps of binding arbitration. However, it is appropriate and necessary that they have role in the process in advisory arbitration.
- Be careful of language that has a questionable legal foundation. For example, in one contract that I reviewed, a section entitled HIV/AIDS Confidentiality, states "[a]ny infected member is encouraged to notify the Superintendent or principal." This establishes language with tacit pressure for an individual to disclose a condition, which is confidential. The more puzzling language follows, "The District shall not discriminate against the infected member without cause." If there is cause is it discrimination? Under what conditions would the school district discriminate?

I was left wondering why this language was even negotiated. On top of it the section states that any breach of confidentiality "is subject to legal action by the member and the Association." This appears to give the Association standing to sue, but for what harm to the Association? What if it is a member of the union who reveals the confidential information, has the Association been harmed? It is clear that the employee who had his/her confidentiality breached would be harmed.

A close reading of the existing contract is important for preparing for the next contract.

Bargaining is hard work. It requires preparation, organization, deft interpersonal skills, integrity, a willingness to check your ego at the door, and a focus on the relationship that will exist after the bargaining has been completed. I finish this section on nuts and bolts with a few tips that I picked up from others and ones that I learned through my time at the table bargaining a contract and away from the table implementing the contract.

- Be straightforward, don't misrepresent or hide the facts.
- Be calm, patient, and tolerant.
- Don't be afraid to say no, but be willing to back it up as to why you have said no.
- Don't believe that you have the corner on truth, there are always things to learn from others.
- Your good word is one of the things that you own, protect it and use it wisely.
- When you have made a mistake at the table, given wrong information, take responsibility at the table. Saying "I made a mistake" protects your good word in that others will know that there is integrity behind it and a genuine desire to be accurate and fair. It is what you would want to hear from others.
- Don't give a last offer unless it is the last offer. You can't have more than one last offer.
- Be flexible with strategy and options but protect the interests you seek at the table.
- At the public sector bargaining table, you do not represent yourself, you represent the constituency who asked you to bargain for them, either labor or management.
- Be cognizant of the conflict of interests that exists and try to expand the community of interests that also exists.

NOTES

1. Frederick M. Hess and Martin R. West, *A better bargain: Overhauling teacher collective bargaining for the 21st century* (Cambridge, MA: Harvard University, Program on Education Policy & Governance, n.d.): 9.

2. Robert A. Gorman, *Basic text on labor law: Unionization and collective bargaining* (St. Paul MN: West Publishing Co., 1976): 399.

3. For an example of the legislative requirement to bargain in good faith in New Hampshire see RSA 273-A:3 Obligation to Bargain.—I. It is the obligation of the public employer and the employee organization certified by the board as the exclusive representative of the bargaining unit to negotiate in good faith. "Good faith" negotiation involves meeting at reasonable times and places in an effort to reach agreement

on the terms of employment, and to cooperate in mediation and fact-finding required by this chapter, but the obligation to negotiate in good faith shall not compel either party to agree to a proposal or to make a concession.

Furthermore, in Illinois the public sector collective bargaining reads in pertinent part: P.A. 84-832 Section 10 Duty to bargain. (a) An educational employer and the exclusive representative have the authority and the duty to bargain collectively as set forth in this Section. Collective bargaining is the performance of the mutual obligations of the educational employer and the representative of the educational employees to meet at reasonable times and confer in good faith with respect to wages, hours, and other terms and conditions of employment, and to execute a written contract incorporating any agreement reached by such obligation, provided such obligation does not compel either party to agree to a proposal or require the making of a concession.

4. William Ury, *The power of a positive no: How to say no and still get to yes* (New York: Bantam, 2007): 7.

5. Roger Fisher and William Ury, *Getting to yes: Negotiating agreement without giving in* (New York: Penguin Books, 1981): 148.

6. Permission to use "An elegant solution for the negotiated agreement" was granted by its author, Richard Fossey, professor, University of North Texas, Denton, Texas, on January 3, 2009, via e-mail.

7. I heard this argument from site administrators that they don't want to be at the table because it may pit them against their teachers. I understand the argument but I reject it. I am a former assistant principal and principal and know that the requirements of the position often place the administrator in a position where he or she must confront teachers who disagree with the position of the school district. Supporting the position of the school board/superintendent is part of the job of being a member of the leadership team. There is little difference, in my opinion, for a school administrator to support the position of the school district at the bargaining table, at the school site, or in public. Argue in private, but support in public is a good refrain for school administrators. Ruben L. Ingram lists fifteen ways to involve principals in negotiations ("Negotiating away barriers to educational opportunity," in *Leadership* 33 (2004): 29).

8. Linda Kaboolian, *Win-win labor management collaboration in education: breakthrough practices to benefit students, teachers, and administrators* (Mt. Morris, IL: Education Week Press, 2005): 24.

9. This concern is supported by research by Linda Babcock, Xianghong Wang, and George Lowenstein, "Choosing the wrong pond: Social comparisons in negotiations that reflect a self-serving bias," in *The Quarterly Journal of Economics*, 111 (1996): 1–18, who found that school districts and unions in Pennsylvania chose comparison groups in ways that advanced their positions rather than providing neutral data points to support bargaining.

10. E-mail correspondence with Danielle Bolduc (June 8, 2009).

11. E-mail correspondence with Travis Nadeau (June 17, 2009).

12. The comparison consists of fifteen diametrically opposed statements that differentiate dialogue from debate that were adapted to studying collective bargaining.

For a listing of Sheldon Berman's comparison Dialogue and Debate items, see http://www.globallearningnj.org/global_ata/a_comparison_of_dialogue_and_debate.htm

13. Michael R. Jette, *Exploring table talk: Does dialogue or debate correspond to success and satisfaction in teacher collective bargaining?* Unpublished doctoral dissertation, Durham, NH: University of New Hampshire, 2005): 119. The debate/dialogue statements used in the research are found on pages 118 and 119.

14. Ibid. 87.

15. Ibid. 91.

16. Todd A. DeMitchell and Richard Barton, "Collective bargaining and its impact on local educational reform efforts." *Educational Policy* 10 (1996): 372.

17. *Appeal of Tamworth Educational Support Personnel Association*, Case No. 2007-0339, (March 24, 2008) *slip op.*

18. William L. Sharp, *Winning at collective bargaining: strategies everyone can live with* (Lanham, MD: The Scarecrow Press, Inc., 2003): 78.

Chapter 8

The Future of Professional Relations

> It's time to consider new and different models of labor-management relations that are more conducive to collaboration and less adversarial. Our mutual responsibility is to do all we can to ensure that all our students succeed.[1]

Labor relations encompasse policies, politics, and practices; it is more than the relationship between two individuals who have a super ordinate and subordinate relationship to each other in a work setting. Schools are people intensive enterprises. Thus, labor relations with its three dimensions are pervasive in today's modern school system whether or not there is a union presence. A union presence within a school system that has collective bargaining adds complexity to the labor relations. And "it has gone largely unexamined by scholars and analysts."[2] It is this complexity and the lack of analysis that has been the focus of this book.

Labor relations involve the development, implementation, and enforcement of policies that define rights and responsibilities in the workplace. These policies enforce conformance with applicable state and federal laws as well as establishing the conditions under which the employee works. This discussion focuses on a specific policy type instrument-a bilaterally collectively bargained contract between the exclusive representative (union) of a defined employee group and the management of their employer that defines, the wages, benefits, and the terms and conditions of the employee group.

There are politics in labor relations because there are "enduring differences, scarce resources, and interdependence."[3] Enduring differences include a conflict of interest; it also means that individuals, without regard to labor/management orientations will often disagree on interpretations, facts, and truth. This human condition plays out in labor relations as well as in other aspects of life. Politics involves the use of power, and coalition building to secure a "fair" portion of the scarce resources. The interdependence of teachers and administrators is recognized in the use of the inclusive term "educators." It is also clear in the research and in the world of the schools that educators, teachers and administrators need each other's support and assistance to perform their professional activities in the best interests of students. There is a community of interest in the politics of labor relations in education.

Finally, policy and politics provides the "what" of labor relations, but those must be developed and instituted through the "how" of labor relations. This is the practice of labor relations. The practices of bargaining a contract and implementing a contract reinforces the type of relationship that is sought by both labor and management—trust and mistrust, us and them, conflict and cooperation, win and loss, are some of the outcomes of practices that establish the relationship.

This last chapter will look to the future of the policy, politics, and practices of education. We can no longer continue to replicate our system of labor relations. We can do it differently. Unions in our schools are not fading away as they are in the private sector workplaces; they are robust and are influential. Unions and collective bargaining play a role in our educational system in large part because education is labor intensive; an important public undertaking that is built around people coming together to create and maintain a community for a purpose—education of our youth. The NEA and the AFT are legitimate, well entrenched, and are perceived by its members as providing a necessary service for them. The relationship between teachers and administrators, between labor and management will endure in one form or another, positive or negative, but it can be done differently. This chapter will offer points for both labor and management to consider.

BREAKING THE INDUSTRIAL UNION TEMPLATE

Teachers labor but they are not laborers. The concept of the regulated workplace that a contract can capture in a standard form through a negotiated contract is inadequate for our classrooms and schools. We must reduce or break the hold of an ill-fitting model and replace it with a more flexible one.

Strikes, work to rule, filing grievances as a tactic to leverage management to meet the demands of the union are associated with the industrial labor model. They may be effective as a counterbalance to lockouts, but the public schools serve the public and thus management cannot withhold this critical governmental service through a lockout as part of a labor dispute in an effort to leverage the union. Similarly, public schools cannot relocate to other towns, states, or countries; it cannot outsource teaching to a less costly location with lowered wages. The industrial union model does not fit and efforts must be made to reduce the impact of this model on public education.

Specifically, the following are good beginning points for reducing the industrial labor hold on education:

Us-and-Them

The us-and-them established by a decades old model of labor relations no longer works in business and has never worked in education. The rhetoric that sustains the distinction between educators should be reduced. The us-and-them dichotomy must make room for "we." This involves both teachers and administrators reconceptualizing the relationship and acting on that new view. This, however, does not mean that there will no longer be a conflict of interest. There will always be some conflict of interest. It does mean that educators allow for the "we" of a community of interest to be just as visible and just as influential as the us-and-them, the conflict of interests of collective bargaining. The us-and-them model tends to exaggerate difference and supports and needs conflict. Cooperation becomes a lull in the permanence of conflict.

Standardization Versus Flexibility

"The union as an organization must be prepared to 'let go' of standardized and centralized work rules."[4]

The standardizing effect of collective bargaining should be rethought. What aspects of a negotiated contract should include standardization and how do we support flexibility when it is needed to further professional practice. Standardizing work behavior may have the unintended consequence of calling for managing teachers through the policing and enforcement of a contract and while inhibiting the empowering of them. Shedd and Bacharach write, "Rather than negotiating rules that restrict flexibility, [the union] will look for ways to relax restrictions on both teachers and administrators."[5] Professional practice demands flexibility and differential action based on the context of the learning situation.

The standard union work rules found in contracts contribute to an inflexible environment. Innovation seeks to break the mold and contracts tend to define and keep the mold. "One need not be an enthusiastic proponent of school choice to see that individual schools (and the teachers in them) to often enjoy insufficient autonomy as a result of collective bargaining agreements."[6] Charter schools seek innovation in large part by having regulations removed from their school and teachers; this includes release from existing collective bargaining agreements.

In an interesting twist, a charter school in Massachusetts in September of 2008 signed individual authorization cards to organize into a union. "The decision by the 20 teachers at this small elementary school is considered significant in the state's 15-year-old charter movement, which was based in part, on allowing administrators to pursue innovative teaching methods without union intervention."[7] The teachers say that they want a more persuasive voice in educational decisions. But the Chairwomen of the trustees noted that there had been friction around pay and health insurance. Similarly, teachers in the Pennsylvania Online Regional Cyber Charter School voted to unionize.[8] The numbers are small but do they foreshadow a trend?

While there have been growing numbers of charter schools which are unionized, a few (in New York) have taken steps to decertify the union. The Executive Director of three charter schools in Los Angeles stated that the union has helped with some staffing issues before they became a grievance. However, she stated that the drive to unionize the faculty "caused disruptions in the school culture," accompanied by a "breakdown in collegiality," and the "establishment of a firmer line between staff and management" with the "adoption of more formalized procedures."[9] These are some of the very outcomes associated with unionization; us and them and formalization of relationships.

Are the charter school teachers seeking a greater professional role under collective bargaining or are they seeking to protect their bread-and-butter interests through a contract?

A community of professionals cannot easily thrive within the confines of standardized, centralized work rules, like those found in industrial union labor contracts.

If the democratic ideal of professionalism suggests that school boards and principals treat teachers as partners in determining school policy, then it also suggests that unions demand fewer fixed policies regarding curriculum, discipline, and work schedules, and more participatory structures within which teachers can join administrators and members of school boards in shaping these policies.[10]

Transfer through Seniority

One of these inflexible rules that undermine reform efforts is transfer policies that rigidly embrace seniority. Collective bargaining agreements may prevent the assignment of the most appropriate teacher to a school—provisions that some view as antithetical to the attainment of professionalism. Provisions that specify that teachers with higher seniority but have received unfavorable evaluations may claim a right to transfer over a less senior but more qualified teacher emphasizes contract criteria, not professional criteria. For example in Los Angeles, teachers bid on positions much like in the private industrial union sector. The Seattle Education Association apparently recognized the limitation of seniority when it ratified a new contract that traded seniority rights in transfer for greater control over professional activities.[11]

Teachers, in a study by DeMitchell and Barton, rated transfer as the most negative contract section affecting reform. One teacher in the study wrote: "Use of seniority to assign teachers to grade, track, etc.; experience, education, training, etc. for a special grade, etc. just doesn't count! The senior teachers can just grab anything they want."[12] Interestingly, in the same study, principals also rated this section of the contract as the one most negatively affecting school reform efforts, and building union representatives rated it as the second most positive section after the evaluation section. The difference in view between teachers and principals with union representatives is stark. Rigid seniority may be a union goal but not a goal of teachers and administrators.

School administrators who make decisions such as transfer, without regard for seniority face the challenge of demonstrating that their decision was not arbitrary or a showing of favoritism. This is a legitimate concern. A 17-year veteran teacher who sat on the Board of the United Teachers of Los Angeles summed the issue in the following way, "Workers fought for seniority rights because there was a problem with managers trying to curry favor with certain folks. And that certainly has not gone away."[13] In an interesting twist to the debate over seniority and favoritism, a teacher of the year nominee was laid off based on seniority just prior to the final decision of who will be the New Hampshire Teacher of the year.[14] In this case seniority trumped a finding of excellence.

This concern places the onus on administrators to use any relaxation in the use of seniority to show that the transfer decision was unbiased, neutral and based on defensible criteria. However, the union cannot hide behind ancient history of past wrongs by administrators who may no longer work in the school district that bears no relation to the current administrators or current history. A past wrong may no longer be a current problem.

Protection

Unions are often associated with the defense of its least competent members to the detriment of the competent and the profession as a whole. Teachers take pride in their work. Most are troubled by the presence of incompetent teachers in their school building. One union building representative commented, "We have, on our staff, a few people who should leave teaching, perhaps 2 or 3 out of 70. It has been difficult to remove them due to contract language."[15]

Teacher unions are caught in a dilemma, they must provide representation for teachers, even the incompetent ones, yet their members want to only work with competent colleagues. The union must be seen by its membership as protecting their own, yet they are aware of the public perception that they protect incompetent teachers to the detriment of children and the community. Compounding this challenge, Johnson notes, "For most teachers, being part of a good school took precedence over union membership."[16] Similarly, DeMitchell and Cobb identified the concern of teachers that the union provides "blind protection" for teachers.[17]

Placing the protection of union members without regard for competence in the classroom is to elevate the needs of the employee over the needs of the recipient of the professional service. A union that seeks a place at the policy table too easily becomes perceived as an issue partisan, like other issue partisans, seeking a narrow agenda within the policy discussion of the public good of education if it pursues blind protection. The focus should be the entitlement of an education for students and not a job for adults.

Unions must provide protection for the due process rights of teachers. They do not have to, nor should they protect the incompetent. Unions protect the process by which incompetence is addressed so that the problem can be identified and addressed fairly. Blind protection ill serves the profession; fair protection is necessary.

The need for fairness in employee discipline is self-evident. Al Shanker, the driving force for the AFT, stated, "We fought to have due process, to give to teachers a fair trial. We did not fight to protect incompetence."[18] Can unions move from the industrial labor model, which calls for the defense of its least competent members to a professional model, which seeks to protect the public from incompetence in its ranks? They must.

The following section explores this challenge.

PROFESSIONAL UNIONISM

The problem, of course, is that schools are utterly dependent on teachers not acting like industrial workers.[19]

The lead Commentary in *Education Week* by Charles T. Kerchner in 1988 was entitled "A 'New Generation' of Teacher Unionism." Kerchner foresaw an emerging new type of union one willing to assume part of the responsibility for garnering respect for public education, improving the schools, and making teaching a profession.[20] Nine years later another lead Commentary in *Education Week* was entitled "The 'New Teacher Unions.'" Koppich, Kerchner, and Weeres wrote, "the unions must begin to move beyond their success at negotiating salary, benefits, and other labor-related issues to organize the teaching part of teaching."[21] Nine years and no change, change is hard to achieve.

Why has the discussion of a professional union faded, like old ink, from the discussion of labor relations? Julia Koppich notes this change writing that "new Unionism has all but disappeared from the NEA agenda."[22] Has the old style industrial unionism reasserted itself? Possibly as a union response to tough economic times—scarce resources heightening competition from different fronts— a retrenchment of labor gains and influences through legislation have combined to cause them hunker down into a more defensive posture. The response to pull back and protect what one has is a recognized response.

Research by the RAND Corporation underscores this response when unions are perceived as moving away from protecting self-interests the membership becomes restless and often searches for new leadership that will "take on" on management.[23] Unions turning away from professional unionism may well be returning to their knitting—a more industrial union.

A hunkered down union misses opportunities. It is hard to see possibilities in the distance when your head is tucked into your neck for protection. Education is not well served when a major player has pulled back. All players must be pushing forward.

We must return to the discussions and the pursuit of professionalizing teaching and adapting the labor relations that in large part defines the conditions under which professional practice occurs. Both unions and management must see the possibilities. In conjunction with reducing the effects of the industrial union model, unions must pursue a different model/paradigm for their part of the labor relations model. Management must dismantle those obstacles to a new model as unions change and seek the expanded community of interest. In many ways, both unions and management should seek to transfer labor relations into professional relations with an acknowledgement of the legitimacy of conflicts of interest and a desire to expand the community of professional interests. A professional union does not abdicate its responsibility to serve the interests of its members; it seeks to broaden what the interests are of its members.

Not Pulling Back, but Pushing Forward

A good beginning point is to return to the past. There was a push for a more professional union a decade ago, and as noted above the dialogue has dropped off the agenda. The discussion below revisits the professional union with a hope to rekindle the discussion.

Don Cameron, Executive Director of the NEA, set the tone for a more professional union when he wrote "teachers and teacher organizations must take greater responsibility for the quality of the teaching force,"[24] a goal of evaluation systems. President Bob Chase soon followed suit a couple of months later in an address to the National Press Club in Washington, D.C. He outlined a new charter for the NEA, one, which would pursue an aggressive agenda of excellence and reform.

After acknowledging that the NEA had often sat on the sidelines of change, nay saying and blocking uncomfortable changes "to protect the narrow interests of our members, and not to advance the interests of students and schools"[25], he vowed a change to lead reform, to be in the vanguard. To accomplish this change, he discussed the need for a new union-management relationship in public education—the industrial-style adversarial tactics simply are not suited for reform he argued.

The NEA must not only be concerned with teachers, it must be concerned with teaching as well. He asserted that the traditional bread-and-butter union agenda of better wages, benefits, terms and conditions of employment remain critical, but they are narrow and inadequate for the future. The narrow bread-and-butter view does not best serve the interests of students and schools. "After all, America's public schools do not exist for teachers and other employees. They do not exist to provide us with jobs and salaries. Schools do exist for the children—to give students the very best . . . beginning with a quality teacher in every classroom."[26]

Specifically, Chase called for the following changes:

- "School quality—the quality of the environment where students learn and where our members work—must be our responsibility as a union.
- The fact is that while the majority of teachers are capable and dedicated—professionals who put children's interests first—there are indeed some bad teachers in America's schools. And it is our job as a union to improve these teachers or—that failing—to get them out of the classroom.
- Quality must begin at home—within our own ranks. If a teacher is not measuring up in the classroom—to put it baldly, if there is a bad teacher in one of our schools—then we must do something about it."
- To parents and the public, NEA pledges to work with you to ensure that every classroom in America has a quality teacher. This means we accept our responsibility to assist in removing teachers—that small minority of teachers—who are unqualified, incompetent, or burned out."[27]

As part of his agenda for the NEA to take responsibility for teaching as well as teachers, Chase called for a change in collective bargaining goals.

Bread-and-butter is not forgotten or ignored in his model, it is joined by professional responsibility. The challenge of professionalism and unionism has been discussed previously. The fact that it is a tangled relationship does not mean that it would better if it were unraveled.

In support of his mission to organize schools for excellence, Chase stated that "instead of contracts that reduce flexibility and restrict change, we-and our schools—need contracts that empower and enable."[28] It appears that he is supporting the idea that contracts should not hold rigidly to the tenets of standardization and centralization, an outcome of collective bargaining. A professional needs flexibility to render the best service, schools also need flexibility, the ability to be nimble to adapt the rapid changes brought by high speed technology, a shrinking world, and shifts in demographics bring to the schoolhouse gate. A large contract that tries to account for all contingencies of a complex workplace like a school and its classrooms spins a web of rules that too often traps and does not release actions that are needed.

Silent Ally—Public Adversary

A move to a professional union challenges what unions do. DeMitchell described the challenge of speaking for both teachers and teaching by discussing the dual role of unions acting as a silent ally and a public adversary.[29] The move away from industrial unionism towards professional unionism, seeks a new balance of rights and obligations for its members, and attempts to move the union from being insular to redefining its interest as consistent with the public's interest. A reinvented union must emphasize its new role by moving from being a silent ally and public adversary to acting as a public ally for professional practice and a public adversary ensuring basic fair treatment of its members and the community's teachers through the implementation of due process and a bilaterally negotiated agreement that seeks appropriate wages, benefits, and terms and conditions of employment.

The union must concomitantly convince its members that a concern for the profession does not mean giving up its traditional role of securing the bread-and-butter issues of bargaining, especially the issue of job security. The focus moves from security, which too often becomes protection of the individual at all costs to protecting the process. This is not an easy challenge to meet.

Some teacher unions have responded to this dilemma by acting as silent allies and public adversaries.

Many school administrators have complained bitterly about the role of unions and collective bargaining when it comes to dismissing incompetent teachers. One principal in the DeMitchell and Barton study wrote, "Poor teachers are protected too much. Cannot get rid of—protected by tenure and local contract."[30] Another administrator commented:

> Our union contract makes it difficult to get rid of teachers. The evaluator must announce every visit in advance; only those visits may be used in the evaluation. The union will file grievances if the district tries to fire a teacher.[31]

In spite of this view, many school administrators have found that they can work with union leaders behind the scenes to induce incompetent teachers to leave. Bridges documented instances where the union was helpful. One California administrator stated, "The union's role is critical in counseling a teacher out. Of the five percent that get counseled out, 75 percent are with the help of the union."[32] Another administrator declared, "I have a good relationship with the district rep, and he helps me work out programs of resignation for the poorest teachers in this district. Without him, my job would be far more difficult."[33] An example of the union moving form silent ally to public ally in support of professional practice is Peer Assistance and Review Programs discussed earlier.

My administrative experience in California confirms that union presidents and paid union staff members positions have been beneficial at times when I have needed to take disciplinary action against an employee. They acted as a silent ally on occasion, protecting the best interests of students and teaching. They were not interested in unthinking, reflexive protection at any cost. They advocated for the teacher to ensure that the process was fair and that the truth could be found. There were times when the union was more effective as the silent ally while holding my feet to the public fire of fairness. Both of us understood the necessity of the public/private split.

Unions can be both private allies and public adversaries when the issue is teacher discipline. Its public role has been the communication of its support of the teacher facing potential disciplinary action so as to show the membership that their union is on the ball protecting them. When there is no concern or little concern for teaching due process protection and not the truth about the charges or the impact of the teacher's actions on the students, the school becomes the lodestone of union action. Blind protection ill-serves professionalism.

For example, a teacher phoned in a bomb threat to an elementary school during a teacher strike in Sunnyvale, California. The teacher pled no contest to a charge of falsely reporting a bomb threat. He believed that a visual count of evacuating students would challenge the school district's report of school attendance levels. The teacher served jail time for the criminal offense. The school district moved to dismiss the teacher for unprofessional and immoral conduct. The case was argued all the way to the California Court of Appeals. The court endorsed an arbitrator's characterization of the conduct when it wrote:

> We view the phoning in of bomb threats as one of the lowest forms of human activity, roughly equivalent to arson and rape. They are similar because in all three situations, an individual is willing to jeopardize the interests of others— perhaps even the lives of others—for his own immediate gratification.[34]

Despite this sentiment, the teacher won and the school district had to pay $7,000 in attorney's fees to the teacher.

Will a reinvented union concerned with the profession of teaching and the commonwealth of education support a teacher who willingly commits a criminal act that endangers schoolchildren? How will a reinvented union react to this situation; will job protection be placed before the interests of children and the public? DeMitchell and Fossey raise the question if the Sunnyvale teacher can retain his job, do we have much hope for removing the incompetent. "Schools can be great places for adults—annual raises, good health insurance, and job protection so good that even a teacher who falsely reports a bomb in a school can escape the consequences of his actions."[35] But shouldn't they first be great places for students?

An attendant issue challenging unions as it speaks for teaching and helps to purge our schools of its few incompetent teachers is its duty of fair representation. When a union has been elected as the exclusive representative of the employees, it owes its members a duty of fair representation. This duty includes the negotiating process, contract administration of an existing agreement, and the administration of an employee's grievance under a collective bargaining agreement.[36] While the United States Supreme Court in *Humphrey v. Moore* stated that unions have a duty to represent employees in an honest manner, without fraud or deceit, that duty has limits.[37] Unions are given considerable discretion regarding what claims to press to grievance and arbitration. They do not have to take every employee grievance through all of the grievance steps and on to arbitration.

The union violates the duty of fair representation when its conduct is arbitrary, discriminatory, or is undertaken in bad in faith.[38] In other words, a union can decide which grievances to pursue and how far to pursue them as long as they do not discriminate against a particular employee. A union has the right to investigate a grievance and gather information in order to make an informed choice. McKinney's research in this area found that it is extremely difficult for individual employees to win fair representation cases against their union. He concludes that "courts are highly deferential to the decisions of unions made during negotiations, contract administration and the grievance process."[39]

The duty of fair representation for its membership should not prove to be a major legal hurdle for the NEA as it pursues its agenda of professionalism. As long as a union is not discriminating against a particular employee and its involvement in the evaluation process, as contemplated by peer review, yields supportable data that an employee should be terminated, it should be shielded from a lawsuit of fair representation. This concern should not deter a union from taking this important step toward speaking for the profession in a meaningful way. The legal concern of a union about a lawsuit is no greater than that faced daily by school administrators who are trying to do their job of proper supervision in order to provide accountability and improvement in instruction, major goals of evaluation.

THE FUTURE

The future of labor relations in education involves choices of policies, politics, and practices. Two basic truths are a foundation for these choices of what policies to pursue, what is traded off and who gains and who shares power through politics, and what practices will be implemented as a result of the politics in pursuit of what policies. First, providing for an educated citizenry is one of the most important functions of government. Second, elementary and secondary education is delivered through the work of people; it is people intensive. Students stand at the core of education but teachers stand at the crossroads that lead from the core to the conception of an educated person.

A consequence of these truths is that in order to provide an effective educational system government needs qualified individuals working in the best interests of students. The labor relations of those qualified individuals and their employer plays an important role in the delivery of the professional service of assessment and teaching. Because the majority of public schools deliver education in a unionized environment, the work of unions and the effects of collective bargaining influence public education; labor relations are structured around the relationship between unions and management.

For too long this relationship has been grounded in the industrial labor model. The consequences of this model have not been good for education. Unions provide a legitimate service, one that teachers clearly value and want. While they may not identify with unions as part of their daily work, they want the protection that they believe unions provide. There will always be a conflict of interest but there is also a community of interest that needs to vigorously pursued.

I conclude with the following observations:

- Labor relations must emphasize the relations part of the term. Once the grievance is settled, the contract signed, the conflict resolved we have the educators in the school who need to work together, and in most instances want to work together. The relationship between people who must work together must not get lost in the labor relations built on an industrial model that separates more than it brings together.
- Labor and management must work to ameliorate the negative impact of the industrial labor model. The challenge for teachers and their unions is to reconcile professionalism and unionism, service to other and self-interest. Administrators face a similar challenge in that they treat teachers as "employees" during bargaining and contract administration, and as valued professionals on curricular and instructional matters. These challenges must be reconciled.
- The union must be able to move beyond the self-interest of its membership but still meet that self-interest. It must be able to stand tall for what is right for the profession and the community and set aside the expedient of just being an advocate for its membership. It is a fine line that unions walk to transform themselves into a professional union. Management must assist in this effort. This is not a singular journey, but rather a journey of educators. The need for a new model is clear; the old one does not work. That does not mean that it will be easy to fashion a new model from which to transform labor relations to professional relations.
- The bargaining table is a legitimate place for both labor and management to pursue their interests. Because there is a community of interests and not just a conflict of interests, the table must not be viewed as disconnected from the rest of the places that educators interact. Both parties, labor and management, may come to the table separately, but they are joined in many ways after leaving the table.
- We must find ways to replicate the concept of good faith required in bargaining and make it part of the regular relationships between educators.
- Neither side should be involved in practices at the bargaining table that attack and demean people and then expect that the behavior which targeted individuals can be forgotten with an understanding that the table is somehow a special place devoid of consequences for personal attacks. The table should not be a place for demonizing. "The public sport of union bashing and administrator trashing will no longer work in a new age of professionalism."[40] Confidence in public education is destroyed both inside and outside the schoolhouse gate when the public is left with the impression that the inept are leading the callous and indifferent.
- We must find ways through working with teachers and the union to consistently strive to change community perceptions to coincide with the reality that educators are members of a learned profession. Once again pursuing

the tenets of a professional union is more than worthwhile; it is necessary. The tension between teacher as professional and teacher as member of an industrial style union must be reduced.

There are no silver bullets, no magic incantations, changing the policies, politics, and practices of the labor relations in education is hard work. If it were easy we would have done it already. Each school district and each side at the bargaining table decides whether the effort to search for new ways and new relationships is important and needed. Hopefully this book helps to provide some compass bearings for the difficult road ahead.

NOTES

1. Adam Urbanski and Clifford B. Janey, "A better bargain," in *Education Week* (May 23, 2001). Site visited May 23, 2001, at http://edweek.org/ew/ewstory .com?siug-5/urbanskin20

2. Jane Hannaway and Andrew J. Rotherham, "Conclusion," in Jane Hannaway and Andrew J. Rotherham (Eds.), *Collective bargaining in education: Negotiating change in today's schools* (Cambridge, MA: Harvard Education Press, 2006): 257.

3. Lee G. Bolman and Terrence E. Deal, *Reframing organizations: Artistry, choice, and leadership* (San Francisco: Jossey-Bass, 1991): 206.

4. Julia E. Koppich, "Getting started: A primer on professional unionism," in Charles Taylor Kerchner and Julia E. Koppich, *A union of professionals: Labor relations and educational reform* (New York: Teachers College Press, 1993): 202.

5. Joseph B. Shedd and Samuel B. Bacharach, *Tangled hierarchies: Teachers as professionals and the management of schools* (San Francisco: Jossey-Bass Publishers, 1991): 168.

6. Hannaway and Rotherham, *supra*, note 2, 259.

7. James Vaznis, "Teachers unionize at charter school, a first for Mass," In the *Boston Globe* (November 26, 2008): A10.

8. *NSBA Legal Clips*, "Teachers at Pennsylvania cyber charter school are the first to unionize," National School Board Association (June 25, 2009): 8.

9. Stephen Sawchuck, "Unions set sights on high-profile charter-network schools," in *Education Week*, 1 (June 10, 2009): 14.

10. Amy Gutman, *Democratic education* (Princeton, NJ: Princeton University Press, 1987): 83–84.

11. Brad Keller, "Seattle teachers approve tentative contract with broad new evaluation, hiring policies," in *Education Week* (September 17, 1997), 8.

12. Todd A. DeMitchell and Richard M. Barton, "Collective bargaining and its impact on local educational reform efforts." *Educational Policy* 10 (1996): 375.

13. Jeff Archer, "Districts targeting seniority in union contracts," in *Education Week* (April 12, 2000): 5.

14. Patrick Cronin, "Teacher of year nominee laid off: Union seniority rule enacted as school cuts jobs." *Portsmouth [NH] Herald* April 27, 2009): A1, A2.

15. DeMitchell and Barton, *supra* note 12.

16. Susan Moore Johnson, *Teacher unions in schools* (Philadelphia: Temple University Press, 1984): 163.

17. Todd A. DeMitchell and Casey D. Cobb, "Teacher as union member and teacher as professional: The voice of the teacher." *Education Law Reporter* 220 (2007): 25–38.

18. Kathy Checkley, "The new union: Helping teachers take a lead in educational reform." *Education Update*, Association for Supervision and Curriculum Development (August 1996): 3.

19. Charles Taylor Kerchner and Julia E. Koppich, "Organizing around quality: The frontiers of teacher unionism," in Tom Loveless (Ed.) *Conflicting Missions/ Teacher Unions and Educational Reform*. Washington, DC: Brookings Institution Press, 2000): 284 (emp. in orginal).

20. Charles T. Kerchner, "A 'new generation' of teacher unionism," in *Education Week* 26 (January 20, 1988): 30.

21. Julia E. Koppich, Charles Taylor Kerchner, and Joseph G. Weeres, "The 'new teacher unions,'" in *Education Week* 60, 43 (April 9, 1997): 60.

22. Julia E. Koppich, "The as-yet-unfulfilled promise of reform bargaining: Forging a better match between the labor relations system we have and the educational system we want," in Jane Hannaway and Andrew J. Rotherham, "Conclusion," in Jane Hannaway and Andrew J. Rotherham (Eds.), *Collective bargaining in education: Negotiating change in today's schools* (Cambridge, MA: Harvard Education Press, 2006): 221.

23. Lorraine M. McDonnell and Anthony Pascal, *Teacher unions and educational reform* (Santa Monica, CA: RAND, April 1988).

24. Don Cameron, "The role of teachers in establishing a quality-assurance system," in *Phi Delta Kappan* 78 (1996): 227.

25. Bob Chase, "The new NEA: Reinventing teacher unions for a new era. Remarks before the National Press Club," Washington, DC (February 7, 1997), p. 3. Site visited June 28, 1997, at http://www.nea.org/.

26. Ibid.

27. Ibid.

28. Ibid.

29. Todd A. DeMitchell, "A reinvented union: A concern for teaching not just teachers," in *The Journal of Personnel Evaluation in Education* 11 (1998): 255–268.

30. DeMitchell and Barton, *supra* note 11, 375.

31. Edwin M. Bridges, *The incompetent teacher: The challenge and response* (Philadelphia: The Falmer Press, 1986): 90.

32. Ibid. 91.

33. Ibid.

34. *Board of Education of Sunnyvale Elementary School District v. Commission of Professional Competence*, 162 Cal. Rptr. 590, 593 (Cal. Ct. App. 1980).

35. Todd A. DeMitchell and Richard Fossey, *The limits of law-based school reform: Vain hopes and false promises* (Lancaster, PA: Technomic Publishing Co. Inc., 1997): 89.

36. Joseph R. McKinney, "The duty of fair representation: What the courts do in education cases." *Education Law Reporter* 116 (1997): 9–17.

37. *Humprey v. Moore*, 375 U.S. 335 (1967).

38. *Vaca v. Sipes*, 386 U.S. 171 (1967).

39. McKinney, *supra* note 36.

40. DeMitchell, *supra* note 29, 265.

Chapter 9

Glossary with Some Comments

AGENCY SHOP: A requirement that all employees in the union unit pay dues or fees to the union to defray the costs of providing representation. (U.S. Office of Personnel Management. Site visited December 31, 2008, at http://www.opm.gov/lmr/glossary/glossarya.asp#AGENCY%20SHOP)

ARBITRATION: At its core, arbitration is a form of dispute resolution. Arbitration is the private, judicial determination of a dispute, by an independent third party. It is an alternative to court action. It is either advisory—either party can reject the opinion—or binding—in which case both parties must accept the decision. (Site visited December 31, 2008, at http://www.mediate.com/articles/grant.cfm)

CAUCUS: This is a timeout from the table. Either party may call a caucus. I recommend that the party who calls the caucus give the other side an approximate amount of time that they plan to be away from the table. If the length of time exceeds the stated amount of time, it is best to inform the other party. Caucusing in this manner treats the time of the party with respect.

When a member of a bargaining team calls for a caucus, the chief spokesperson, or the person speaking for them, should immediately stop talking and prepare for the caucus. A caucus can be called to discuss a proposal the other party just submitted or it can be called to stop the flow of the conversation because a team member has a reservation of what is currently taking place.

FAIR REPRESENTATION, DUTY of: The union's duty to represent the interests of all unit employees without regard to union membership. (U.S. Office of Personnel Management. Site visited December 31, 2008, at http://www.opm.gov/lmr/glossary/glossaryf.asp#FAIR%20REPRESENTATION, %20DUTY%20OF)

GOOD FAITH BARGAINING: The duty to approach negotiations with a sincere resolve to reach a collective bargaining agreement, to be represented by properly authorized representatives who are prepared to discuss and negotiate on any condition of employment, to meet at reasonable times and places as frequently as may be necessary and to avoid unnecessary delays, and, in the case of the agency, to furnish upon request data necessary to negotiation. (U.S. Office of Personnel Management. Site visited December 31, 2008, at http://www.opm.gov/lmr/glossary/glossaryg .asp#GOOD%20FAITH%20BARGAINING)

GRIEVANCE: An alleged violation, misapplication, or misinterpretation of a specific section of the collective bargaining agreement. I always wear the grievance hat when a grievance has been submitted.

IMPASSE: When the parties have reached a deadlock in negotiations they are said to have reached an impasse in negotiations If bargaining on any subject is still proceeding impasse cannot be declared. Impasse proceeding typically involves mediation and fact finding. (U.S. Office of Personnel Management. Site visited December 31, 2008, at http://www.opm.gov/lmr/glossary/ glossaryb.asp#BARGAINING%20IMPASSE)

INTEREST ARBITRATION: The arbitrator, instead of interpreting and applying the terms of an agreement to decide a grievance, determines what provisions the parties are to have in their collective bargaining agreement. (U.S. Office of Personnel Management. Site visited December 31, 2008, at http://www.opm.gov/lmr/glossary/glossaryi .asp#INTEREST%20ARBITRATION)

INTEREST BASED BARGAINING: A bargaining technique in which the parties start with (or at least focus on) interests rather than proposals; agree on criteria of acceptability that will be used to evaluate alternatives; generate several alternatives that are consistent with their interests, and apply the agreed-upon acceptability criteria to the alternatives so generated in order to arrive at mutually acceptable contract provisions. The success of the technique depends, in large measure, on mutual trust, candor, and a willingness to share information. (U.S. Office of Personnel Management. Site visited December 31, 2008, at http://www.opm.gov/lmr/glossary/glossaryi .asp#INTEREST-BASED%20BARGAINING)

PAST PRACTICE: Existing practices sanctioned by use and acceptance, that are not specifically included in the collective bargaining agreement. Arbitrators use evidence of past practices to interpret ambiguous contract language. (U.S. Office of Personnel Management. Site visited December 31, 2008, at http://www.opm.gov/lmr/glossary/glossaryp.asp#PAST%20PRACTICE)

PACKAGED PROPOSAL: A proposal that contains more than one section of the contract. It is a package in that the various sections cannot be severed from the whole package by the nonmoving party. In my view packaged proposals work best toward the end of bargaining when the momentum has picked up to ward resolution or the two parties are trying one last ditch effort before declaring impasse.

PROPOSAL: This is a formal statement of one party's proposed language to be inserted into the contract. It is given to the other party at the bargaining table. If a proposal is agreed to by both parties that language is signed off as approved (tentative agreement).

REOPENER CLAUSE: Provisions in the CBA specifying the conditions under which one or either party can reopen for renegotiation the agreement or designated parts of the agreement. The purpose of a reopener is to enable one party to *compel* the other party to renegotiate the provisions covered by the reopener. (U.S. Office of Personnel Management. Site visited December 31, 2008, at http://www.opm.gov/lmr/glossary/glossaryr .asp#REOPENER%20CLAUSE)

RIGHTS ARBITRATION: Rights Arbitration (a.k.a. Grievance Arbitration) deals with the allegation that an existing collective agreement has been violated or misinterpreted. (Site visited December 31, 2008, at http://www .mediate.com/articles/grant.cfm)

SUNSET PROVISION: A sunset provision gives a definite date in which a specific contract section will no longer be in effect. An example is a specific date in which an early retirement provision will no longer be available.

SUPPOSALS: Supposals are different than proposals. A supposal is a strategy used at the bargaining table to get both sides to talk about an issue in a search for a community of interest on the topic. Its goal is to stimulate talking and exploration with a reduced concern about the formality of a proposal.

TENTATIVE AGREEMENT: When agreement has been reached by both parties on a section of the contract, both parties sign an original of the proposal that has been agreed upon. That section of the contract is considered to have been agreed upon. I suggest to management that it prepare the document/proposal that has been agreed upon and that each party retain a signed original for their files. Since management prepares the contract for distribution, it makes the most sense for management to prepare the document subject to union approval.

UNFAIR LABOR PRACTICE: An alleged violation of the state public employment law. An unfair labor practice is heard before the state public employment board, the agency charged with the implementation of the state public employment law.

WATER COOLER NEGOTIATIONS: Sometimes the chief spokesperson for each side will seek to break through a knotty problem. When they informally meet away from the table, at the water cooler to get a drink of water, they can float ideas that they do not want to bring to the table. It is a way to try out different solutions without the constraints of the bargaining table. If successful and they come to an agreement to bring back the idea to their respective teams, they place trust in their counterpart that the water cooler negotiations will not formalized to their detriment. This is a risky undertaking because both are removed from their team. It is a strategy that does not work well in early negotiations but may provide breakthroughs later in negotiations. I have used this strategy when I was a chief spokesperson and my classes often use it.

YELLOW DOG CONTRACT: An employment contract in which the employer forbids the employee to join a labor union as a condition of employment. Yellow-dog contracts are not legally enforceable. (Site visited December 31, 2008, at http://www.nolo.com/definition.cfm/Term/8633A232 -7292-4D40-807A302C91B80A0D/alpha/Y/) It was commonly called yellow dog contract because no sel- respecting dog would sign such a contract.

ZIPPERED CONTRACT: A contract that has no reopeners, consequently it can only be opened by mutual consent of the parties. In other words it is zipped close.

Appendix A

ARROYO WELLS SCHOOL DISTRICT COLLECTIVE BARGAINING SIMULATION

The following simulation, the Arroyo Wells School District Collective Bargaining Simulation, is the driving force in my collective bargaining class. I break the class into two teams: management (Arroyo Wells School District—District) and labor (Arroyo Wells Teachers Association—AWTA). One part of my class is devoted to the academics of labor relations found in the rest of this book and the other part of the class is reserved for the students to work with their team to prepare for bargaining. The two teams prepare for bargaining throughout the semester. The teams receive the simulation below. The back-up materials in the Appendix are not given to them.

One of the challenges of bargaining a contract is knowing what materials/ data is needed. Part of the challenge of bargaining is deciding what data is of the greatest worth to the task at hand. However, since that is not possible in this type of a format I have included the backup materials in the appendices.

I play the role of the constituency for each team—the union president for AWTA and the superintendent for the district. Bargaining teams, as I have discussed previously, do not represent their personal views, interests, and needs. They represent the interests and needs of the constituency they represent at the table. My role of the constituency allows me to work with both teams and to provide support for their bargaining.

The bargaining is expedited. Ten hours (two five-hour sessions) at the end of the semester is reserved for bargaining. No other class activities take place during those times. If the teams wish to meet ahead of time to discuss ground rules or to share their bargaining "interests" I allow time for those

151

discussions. When the bargaining begins I videotape the sessions for analysis at the end of the bargaining class for a debriefing of what worked well and what could have worked better. I have included the debriefing memo from 2009 spring class at the end of this appendix.

The teams work out their own table process/ground rules for bargaining. They call their caucuses and resume when they are ready. They decide whether there will be a chief spokesperson or whether their table talk is ad hoc with all participating, or whether they assign specific issues to individuals.

I sit in on caucuses as often as I can. I also respond to questions from the teams when they are trying out proposals that meet their interests and creatively try to meet the interests of the other party. Outside of my presence, I try to keep the experience as close as possible to the real thing as I can with the simulation.

About half of the time the class settles a contract. However, as I discussed in the introduction, the measure of success of bargaining is not in getting an agreement. The measure of success is the extent to which relations are improved or harmed. As was discussed in the chapter on research, bargaining that is considered problem solving is more effective. In the converse, bargaining that results in a contract, but just adds to the baggage of bad feelings sets the stage for more animosity and a belief that my victory is only achieved at vanquishing the other side.

THE SIMULATION

Arroyo Wells School District is a public school district. It is a kindergarten through twelfth grade district with four elementary schools (K-5), one middle school (6-8), one high school (9-12). There are 2,800 students with 175 certificated faculty members not counting classified staff and administrative staff. The faculty is older with a mean age of 47.

The town of Arroyo Wells is semi-rural. The farms and expanses of woods are giving way to development. The population has been slowly growing with mainly younger professionals and semi-professionals moving in as a means to escape from the metropolitan area. Many of these new families have toddlers or are just starting a family. This shift in population will cause a population bubble to run through the school in the next three to five years. Aside from these newcomers, there is a long-term population that has maintained the power base and they are happy with the way things are and have always been.

The school district enjoys a deserved reputation for excellence. It attracts quality teachers who stay once they have been hired. Few teachers see Arroyo

Wells as a way station as they look for better positions. The district has lower class sizes than many other surrounding school districts and its salary schedule is considered to be quite good. This is a source of pride for residents, parents, and the school district's employees. The schools consistently score at or near the top in state tests.

The town has a population of around 17,000 full time residents. It is located about 30 miles from one of the state's population centers that provide employment for most of the newcomers and some of the established residents. The State University is approximately 15 miles away and provides education opportunities for the faculty.

The socio-economic status of the school district is strong. This is in part because the town is considered an attractive place to live with good schools, an easy commute to employment opportunities, with proximity to a very good state university. The Aid for Dependent Children (AFDC) percentage for Arroyo Wells is seven percent. This compares favorably to the two local school districts, which both the union and management consider to be comparators. Metroville School District has an AFDC percentage of 26 and Happy Valley School District has an AFDC percentage of 15 percent.

The cost of living for the past three years has been 3.75 percent, 3.45 percent, and 3.00 percent. The current cost of living 3.70 and is projected to be steady throughout the year. The town employees in Arroyo Wells have received the following raises during the last three years: Last Year—4.5 percent, year before—4.0 percent, and three years ago—3.75 percent (see Appendix A–3 for comparative pay raises with Metroville School District and Happy Valley School District. The town employees have been perceived as being paid less than the teachers and to have been treated less fairly as the teachers when it comes to salary.

The last contract was finally negotiated with both the superintendent and union president participating in the process. It was a three-year zippered contract with pay raises built in but with no financial escape clause. The contract is expiring. The raises for the three previous years were 4.5 percent, 4.0 percent, and 3.75 percent. Funding from the State is relatively flat and the local population is concerned about rising property tax. Many of the older residents want the school district to hold the line on expenditures, believing that the teachers are overpaid for their "part-time" jobs. However, the newer residents strongly support the schools and the school district. Real estate agents support the schools and routinely point to the schools as a selling point. Consequently, housing prices have risen and developers seek to build in the community.

The high salary and the low class size have combined to strain the financial resources of the school district. The district believes, and is not refuted by the

AWTA, that both of these issues have required that during the last two years the district has had to use funds from its reserve and to delay needed preventive maintenance work on the schools in order to balance the budget.

THE DISTRICT AND AWTA NEGOTIATIONS

Negotiations have been going on for several months with little progress. Both sides have decided to try two days of expedited negotiating sessions in order to try to bring in a contract. If these sessions fail both sides will mutually declare impasse and request a mediator as per state law. Tentative agreement had already been reached on all of the easy items. The difficult items remain. Listed below are the unresolved issues and each side's last position. The unresolved contract sections are found at the end of this chapter as is information on class size, the salary schedule, and abbreviated budget. Other important information needed for bargaining is found in Appendix A.

Each side will develop proposals on each of the following unresolved issues. They can use supposals and water cooler negotiations to augment the proposals.

Salary

The district ended the last two years with reserves of less than five percent. It had some unexpected maintenance issues that overwhelmed its small deferred maintenance budget. In addition, it hired some new teachers because of some increased class sizes. The district received criticism from some of the established community members about paying high salaries with low class sizes thus placing a burden on the taxpayer. The superintendent and Board of Trustees are sensitive to comments about "loose" spending and want to hold the line with this round of bargaining.

In addition, the escalating costs of fringe benefits is placing a strain on the budget. This is especially true since the district currently pays 100 percent of the cost for medical, dental, life, and disability insurance.

Each one percent increase on the salary schedule costs approximately $95,000 in salary and $34,000 in corresponding fringe benefits.

AWTA: The union came down from its original position of 8 percent to its last proposal of 5 percent.

DISTRICT: Management has maintained a 1 percent increase from the beginning of bargaining to its last offer. It has argued that any increase in the ongoing expenditures, such as increases to the salary schedule need to be offset with cost decreases such as decreases to the fringe benefit costs through burden sharing. But, it also knows that it will need to increase the offer, especially if it wants to do retrieval bargaining by having the union move from the district paying 100 percent of fringe benefits costs.

Fringe Benefits

For the current year, AWSD's medical insurance rates rose 14.6 percent. Over the last ten-year period the medical insurance rates rose an average of 12 percent. Last year the rates only rose two percent. Dental insurance has followed a similar pattern with a slightly smaller rise in premiums—three percent this year. Arroyo Wells is the only school district in the surrounding area that pays 100 percent of the medical and dental insurances. Arroyo Wells and the two comparator school districts, Metroville School District and Happy Valley School District pay for life insurance and disability insurance.

AWTA: The union wants to keep the current 100 percent district paid benefits. However, it knows that it is not realistic. The increased costs of fringe benefits erode the amount of new revenue available for salary. The older teachers want a higher salary so that their retirement will increase. They are less concerned with fringe benefits since their children have grown and left home or they do not have children. The younger teachers, especially those with families, want a high salary also, but voice a need for good medical and dental benefits for their family.

DISTRICT: The district has a strong interest in shifting some of the burden of increased fringe benefit costs to the employee. As a show of good faith, the district, through the superintendent, has informed the management team that the district would no longer pay 100 percent of the costs for fringe benefits. They are discussing whether to place a dollar cap on the amount of fringe benefits that the district would pay or whether to move to a percentage that the district pays for insurance with the administration picking up the rest. The two surrounding comparator school districts have burden sharing in their contract. Metroville School District has an 85/15 percent split in which the school district pays 85 percent of medical and dental and the employee pays 15 percent. The percentages stay the same as the cost of insurance rises.

Happy Valley has a dollar amount cap. The cap is for a maximum monthly dollar amount. At his point the dollar cap covers the cost of single coverage for all insurances. However, the cap does not cover all of the costs for the most expensive medical insurance for family. Happy Valley pays $1,500 a month for medical and dental insurance. This covers the most expensive costs for a single subscriber ($31.58 dental & $552.59 for medical = $584.17) for both but does not cover the costs for family ($109.12 dental & $1,492.00 for medical = $1,601.12). Unit members who cover family in these two plans would pay out-of-pocket $101.12 per month. However, if the school district has other insurance options that are less costly, the employee has the option of moving to a lower cost insurance plan during the open enrollment period. A dollar cap forces the Association to negotiate a larger dollar amount for the cap. The District argues that would allow the Association to make reasoned choices between how it wants to distribute limited resources available for salary and fringe benefits.

Extra Duty Salary Schedule

The extra duty salary schedule is based on a formula with a unit value of $310 applied to a sliding scale of units based on the time commitment and the level supervision. For example, the athletic director has a unit value of 4.25 and the middle school yearbook advisor has a unit value of 1.75.

AWTA: The union has proposed that the dollar amount be changed to a percentage of the beginning salary, Step 1 Column A. Its last offer was 1.5 percent of the beginning salary.

DISTRICT: The district has rejected the offer stating that it would constitute an increased cost each year that the beginning salary was increased. Its last position was "no change" to the current contract.

Class Size

AWTA: Has proposed a class size reduction of one student in all categories (see end of simulation contract sections). It asserts that smaller class sizes are necessary for students if they are to meet AYP standards. The union points out that parents strongly support small class size.

DISTRICT: Has proposed an increase in class size of one student for each category. The district asserts that there is no research evidence that reducing class size by one student, given the current class size language, significantly improves student learning. And conversely, they argue that there is no research that supports that an increase of one student will significantly harm student learning. The district views this as not only an educational issue but a financial issue as well. A reduction of class size will necessitate the hiring of more teachers. An increase in class size will slow the hiring of teachers.

Leaves

8.6 Adoption & Child-Rearing Leave A member of the unit (male or female) who wishes to take a personal leave to raise a child immediately following childbirth or upon adoption of a child, may be granted such leave without pay for up to one (1) year.

AWTA: The union wants the leave to be with half pay as if it were a sabbatical.

DISTRICT: States that it is a cost item in a time when the budget is a concern. If the AWTA wants this cost item what is it willing to give up in order to get it? In addition, the District argues that personal leave to raise a child is not like a sabbatical that involves extended study, which benefits the district and its students.

Reassignment Within a School

Language in pertinent part reads:
ARTICLE 10 TRANSFER PROCEDURE.
10.3 Involuntary Transfer

10.31 The District shall seek volunteers prior to making any involuntary transfer/reassignment. If an involuntary transfer/reassignment becomes necessary, the unit member with the least District seniority shall be transferred or reassigned.

Background: Application of 10.31.

In order to reassign one history teacher (#1) at the middle school from 5 periods of 8th grade history to 4 periods of 8th grade history and one period of 7th grade history and there were no volunteers the following would occur. A teacher (#2) at the high school would have to be reassigned for one period to the middle school. A history teacher (#3) at the high school would be reassigned to the one period that missing period of history at the high school level. The course that that teacher was reassigned came from his physical education assignment. The next least senior teacher (#4) to fill that physical education. class has an English credential and is pulled from the English curriculum. The next least senior teacher (#5) who holds a credential in English is at the middle school. That teacher is assigned one period of physical education at the high school. The 7th grade English class which now must be staffed comes from the journalism program. That teacher (#6) is pulled from a journalism class. The other journalism teacher who also holds a credential in English (#7) must now pick up one additional period of journalism thus creating an opening. This teacher does not like teaching the low level 7th grade English class thus does not volunteer. This still creates an opening for an English class which the original teacher who started the fall of the dominos (#1) cannot teach because he does not possess the appropriate credential and is still without his fifth teaching assignment. To fill the English position, a special education teacher (#8) who has dual certification is pulled from his special education class. The next least senior special education teacher teaches at Central Elementary School. Her position at Central is now filled by a 3rd grade teacher (#9) who recently returned to the regular classroom. Teacher (#1) still does not have a position. We have two special education classes in which the teacher must leave for one period a day to cover classes. The bumping can still continue because teacher (#1) does not have an assignment and all other history teachers are very high on the seniority list.

A similar scenario can be played out at the elementary school if a teacher who teaches 3rd grade one year is reassigned to second grade the next year because of a change in student enrollment.

AWTA: The Association stated that they might be willing to trade language changes in the current contract for some acceptable rewording of 10.31. The Director of Personnel stated that the district would not be leveraged into opening up a zippered contract and that the district might force the issue into arbitration. The Director also stated that the feeling of the management team that AWTA was not dealing in a fair manner and that AWTA was just opportunistic which does not breed harmonious labor relations. The issue was still not resolved at the time that negotiations started for the new contract. There are no pending grievances on 10.31 although there are occasional grumbles and threats when some individuals are upset with decisions made my administration

DISTRICT: Several months following the ratification of the contract, the principal of the middle school discussed plans with his staff for the following year's teaching assignments. As in the past, a number of the teachers' assignments would be altered to meet changing student needs. In the past the principal had always had the discretion to make reasonable changes within the confines of an individual's teaching credential. These changes were not considered a violation of the contract but instead a part of doing business. This changed that Spring, two teachers at the school did not like the planned changes and complained strenuously to the principal, AWTA, and the lounge in general. The two teachers eventually filed a grievance citing the new language in 10.31. The teachers contended that the administration could not involuntarily "reassign" them from their present assignment. If a reassignment was necessary the district had to move the least senior district employee. The administration objected vehemently to this interpretation. AWTA backed the two teachers publicly but privately some of the AWTA negotiators stated that that interpretation was never intended. The administration backed down from the intended change at that time, but registered a complaint with AWTA and requested a discussion session to iron out the situation.

The meeting in September of last year did not go well. AWTA contended that they intended the language of that section to apply to any reassignment, even a change from teaching 7th grade history one year to teaching 8th grade history the following year. The district contended that they never would have agreed to such ridiculously confining language had they known the union's interpretation. AWTA countered that the district could use the seniority of the school to implement the language of 10.31. The district responded that that construction was never advanced by the Union and thus, was never intended to be part of it. In addition, the only accepted definition in the contract and through past practice was that seniority was district seniority, the point that the employee started to work for the district. The district does not even keep records specific to how long an employee has been employed at a specific school. It has flatly rejected the idea of altering the concept of seniority from district seniority to school seniority.

The district wants the word reassignment removed from 10.31.

Professional Assignments

7.7 ACTIVITIES/ASSIGNMENTS
Members of the unit shall participate in professional activities and perform professional assignments beyond the regular workday as needed and consistent with past practices of the District.

AWTA: The union has put forward language to remove this section of the contract in each of the last three contracts. Each time they withdrew their proposal to gain other concessions and to get a contract. Over the past five years there have been five grievances filed regarding this section. Each grievance tried to demonstrate that a particular management practice was in violation of this article. Part of their argument was cast along the lines that this language was too vague to be implemented. Four of those grievances originated at the high school and one at the middle school. All five were closely linked in time to upcoming contract negotiations. The grievances typically centered on after school committee work, parent teacher conferences, after school duties. One of the grievances, actually filed under 7.3, was taken to advisory arbitration. Section7.3 was used to try to get around the singular lack of union success with 7.7. The arbitrator upheld the grievance but the board rejected it based on the past practice of 7.7.

DISTRICT: There is no definition of 7.7. It typically has been used to mean that teachers had to attend committee meetings and to meet with parents or administrators. It is invoked very rarely by administration as a rationale for its decisions. Past practice is on the side of management in that when 7.7 has been used its application has been somewhat of an expansive incorporation of several different types of activities. The other key to this issue is that AWTA has given up its position in regards to 7.7 in the past in order to secure a contract. AWTA's desire to remove 7.7 has never formed the basis for impasse in prior negotiations.

The district has consistently refused to remove or change the language. In fact, at several times of frustration at the bargaining table, the district negotiators have remarked that it is the only place where the term professional appears in the contract.

Arbitration

In the past ten years only four grievances have been heard and decided by an arbitrator. In three of the cases the Board accepted the decision of the arbitrator; one of those decisions went against the district. The Board rejected one decision. The issue centered around 7.3 and 7.7. AWUTA argued that mandatory department committee meetings at the high school violated 7.3. The arbitrator agreed. The Board agreed with management that the applicable section was 7.7 and it was controlling because of the long past practice of mandatory departmental meetings.

AWTA: The association wants binding arbitration arguing that it a fair and accepted practice.

DISTRICT: The school board has consistently argued that they were elected by the community and that it would be a dereliction of their duty to turn over decision making to a third party via binding arbitration. The superintendent is achieving some success with the board in getting them to understand that under current state public sector collective bargaining law that a contract that does not have a workable grievance procedure, defined as lacking binding arbitration, allows a grievance to be elevated to an unfair labor practice. Hence, a third party, the public employment relations board, will issue a binding decision. The district may give on this issue but it needs to not just give it away and it must be mindful of "positive assurance" (see the chapter on grievances for an explanation of positive assurance).

Evaluation

12.12 Procedure

(a) Every probationary member of the unit shall be evaluated in writing by his/her immediate supervisor/principal in writing at least no later than February 15.

(b) Any member of the unit who receives a negative evaluation shall, upon request, be entitled to two (2) subsequent observations and a written evaluation of the observations. If the deficiency(ies) noted in the negative have been corrected, the second evaluation shall become part of the unit member's file, and shall be attached to the original evaluation.

(c) The evaluation of members of the unit, except for alleged violation of procedural matters, shall not be subject to the Grievance Procedure.

AWTA: The union is willing to trade the language that the district wants for 12.12 (a) for what it wants for 12.12 (e). However, it is concerned that moving the deadline closer to the mandated state law deadline will negatively impact 12.12 (b) which provides for two additional observations following a negative evaluation.

DISTRICT: The district believes that the February 15th deadline for a written evaluation comes too soon. The state deadline for renominating probationary teachers is April 15th. The administrators want to have an extra month and one-half, to the first of April, for the last written evaluation. They argue that the additional time may make the difference in a positive or negative employment decision. This change, the administration's bargaining team asserts, is in the best interests of the teacher.

AWTA: The association wants to grieve the content of the evaluation not just the procedures used in the evaluation. The union believes that its members need to be protected from incompetent or vindictive administrators. The ability to grieve the content of an evaluation, the union negotiating team asserts, keeps the evaluation honest.

DISTRICT: Management is emphatic in saying no. They believe that it would clearly erode their ability to supervise the faculty. They also assert that an arbitrator may not be an educator and would thus not understand the pedagogy and research that supports evaluations. Consequently, the arbitrator would likely be confined to those elements of labor relations that they understand, such as the procedural aspects of the evaluation which is already protected.

Early Retirement Incentive

Of the two neighboring school districts, only Happy Valley gave any type of an early retirement incentive plan. The plan was offered during the last school year for one time only. The district offered to pay the medical and dental benefits for the employee and his/her spouse up to the maximum cap allowable under the current contract (whatever cap is in the contract each year) to age 65. The employee must have worked in the district for at least 10 years and be at least 55 years of age during the year that he/she retires. Previously, the employee could purchase the insurance at the group rate.

The last collective bargaining agreement had a one-time only early retirement plan. The cost of the Supplemental Early Retirement Plan (SERP) was approximately 20,000 per retiree (it varied according to the employee's salary and years worked in the state) paid out over five years to the contracting company. Six people took advantage of the SERP. All retiree positions were filled. The amount of savings is unknown.

AWTA: The leadership wants an early retirement incentive package. There are a large number (36) of staff members who are at least 55 years old. This is a powerful group of teachers. AWTA also asserts that an incentive that assists high paid teachers to retire will result in a savings to the district when it hires lower paid teachers. The union wants a multi-year incentive arguing that teachers deserve the incentive and should have flexibility in deciding when to accept the incentive and retire.

DISTRICT: The district is not against this proposal, per se, but holds that any early retirement incentive must improve the district's financial condition within five years. In other words, the district has stated that within five years the cost of the incentive must be outweighed by the savings generated by the incentive. The district only wants a one- year incentive arguing that the incentive must be an inducement for teachers to retire earlier than they would have. The district does not save money by giving an incentive to someone who had intended to retire anyway, it argues.

The contract section below reflects the state of bargaining as you prepare for expedited bargaining. The language is the current language. Where "No Change" is indicated that means that the proposals for both the district and the union match with neither seeking a change in the language. All other language is open for negotiations.

Salary Schedule

Year	BA	BA+15	MA	MA+15	MA+30
1	34,121	33,466	38,343	41,740	44,520
2	34,529	36,466	40,064	43,183	46,195
3	36,119	38,688	41,909	45,171	48,292
4	37,784	40,467	43,822	47,252	50,519
5	39,513	42,328	45,851	49,424	52,836
6	41,332	44,266	48,004	51,745	55,318
7	43,292	46,363	50,324	54,243	57,985
8	45,273	48,487	52,868	57,084	61,029
9		50,646	55,508	59,554	63,351
10		52,870	59,058	63,584	66,945
11					69,545

Source: Education Stipend—Added to Base Salary—Cumulative
CAGS/CAS/Ed.S.= $1,000
Ed.D./Ph.D. = $2,500

Longevity Stipend—Added to Base Salary and Education Stipend—Non-Cumulative
12 to 13 years of continuous service in AWSD = $750
14 to 16 years of continuous service in AWSD = $1,500
17 to 19 years of continuous service in AWSD = $2,000
20 to 25 years of continuous service in AWSD = $2,500
26 + years of continuous service in AWSD = $3,000

Class Sizes for the Schools (Special education classes are not counted in this data.)

Mesquite Elementary School (K-5), 405 students

Grade Level	Number of Students	Grade Level	Number of Students
Kindergarten	22	First	23
Kindergarten	24	First	23
Kindergarten	23	First	24

Grade Level	Number of Students	Grade Level	Number of Students
Second	22	Third	24
Second	24	Third	25
Second/Third	20	Third	24

Grade Level	Number of Students	Grade Level	Number of Students
Fourth	25	Fifth	26
Fourth	25	Fifth	25
Fourth	26		

Center School (K-5), 449 students

Grade Level	Number of Students	Grade Level	Number of Students
Kindergarten	23	First	23
Kindergarten	22	First	23
Kindergarten	24	First	23
		First/Second	20

Grade Level	Number of Students	Grade Level	Number of Students
Second	24	Third	24
Second	22	Third	23
Second	23	Third	24

Grade Level	Number of Students	Grade Level	Number of Students
Fourth	25	Fifth	26
Fourth	25	Fifth	25
Fourth	26	Fifth	24

Sierra Vista Elementary School (K-5), 350 students

Grade Level	Number of Students	Grade Level	Number of Students
Kindergarten	21	First	23
Kindergarten	21	First	22
Kindergarten	22	First	22

Grade Level	Number of Students	Grade Level	Number of Students
Second	23	Third	24
Second	23	Third	23
Second	23		

Grade Level	Number of Students	Grade Level	Number of Students
Fourth	25	Fifth	26
Fourth	26	Fifth	26

(Continued)

Class Sizes for the Schools *(Continued)*

Main Street School (K-5) 418 students

Grade Level	Number of Students	Grade Level	Number of Students
Kindergarten	22	First	23
Kindergarten	21	First	22
Kindergarten	22	First	23

Grade Level	Number of Students	Grade Level	Number of Students
Second	22	Third	22
Second	24	Third	23
Second	23	Third	23

Grade Level	Number of Students	Grade Level	Number of Students
Fourth	24	Fifth	26
Fourth	24	Fifth	25
Fourth	24	Fifth	25

Abenaqui Middle School 528 students

Arroyo Wells High School 642 students

Certificated Staff Distribution

Mesquite Elementary School:	17 teachers
Center School:	19 teachers
Sierra Vista Elementary School:	15 teachers
Main Street School:	18 teachers
Abenaqui Middle School:	35 teachers
Arroyo Wells High School	42 teachers
Psychologists:	4
Nurses:	3
Music/Physical Education:	8 for elementary schools
Special Education Teachers:	14
Administrators:	Superintendent Assistant Superintendent for Curriculum Director of Personnel & Labor Relations Director of Business Services 6 principals 2 assistant principals

ARTICLE 6

Grievance Procedure

(The Informal and Level 1 stages of the Grievance Procedure are not contested.)

6.0   No Change

6.1   No Change

6.2   No Change

6.3   No Change

6.31 No Change

6.32 No Change

6.33 No Change

6.34 Level 2 Superintendent

If the aggrieved person is not satisfied with the disposition of his grievance at Level 1, or if no decision has been rendered within five (5) school
days after the presentation of the grievance, he/she may file the grievance in
writing within five (5) school days after the decision at Level 1 or ten (10)
school days after the grievance was presented, whichever is sooner, to the
Superintendent with the objective of resolving the matter.

6.35   Level 3 Advisory Arbitration

(a) If the aggrieved person is not satisfied with the disposition of the grievance at Level 2, or if no decision has been rendered within ten (10)
school days after the grievance was delivered to the Superintendent,
she/he may, within five (5) school days after the decision by the Superintendent or fifteen (15) school days after the grievance was delivered
to the Superintendent, whichever is sooner, request in writing that
the grievance be submitted to advisory arbitration. The Association
shall retain the right to determine whether a grievance may proceed to
arbitration.

(b) Within ten (10) school days after such written notice of submission to
advisory arbitration, the Board and the Association shall attempt to agree
upon a mutually acceptable arbitrator and shall obtain a commitment
from said arbitrator to serve. If the parties are unable to agree upon an
arbitrator or to obtain such a commitment within the specified time, a
request may be made to the American Arbitration Association (AAA) by
either party. The parties shall then be bound by the rules and procedures
of the AAA in the selection of an arbitrator.

(c) The arbitrator so selected shall confer with the representatives of the Board
and the Association and hold hearings promptly and shall issue an award

not later than twenty (20) days from date of the close of the hearings or, if oral hearings have been waived by both parties, then from the date of the submission of final statements and proofs. The arbitrator's recommendation shall set forth his/her findings of fact, reasoning, and conclusions on the issue(s) submitted.

6.36   Level 4

The award of the arbitrator shall be final unless overturned by the Board within thirty (30) days of the rendering of the award. The Board decision of the Board shall be final and binding on the school district.

6.4   Rights of Teachers to Representation

Any aggrieved person may be represented at all stages of the grievance procedure by herself/himself, or, at her/his option, be accompanied by a representative of the Association.

6.5   Rights of Participants

No reprisals of any kind shall be taken by the Board or by any member of the administration against any party in interest, any representative, any member of the Association, or any participants in a grievance by reason of such participation.

ARTICLE 7

Hours of Employment

7.1   No Change

7.2   No Change

7.3   Meetings

Faculty meetings shall not exceed fifteen (15) per year, as needed and shall not exceed one (1) hour in duration, except in cases of emergency. Emergency is defined to mean a sudden unexpected happening, or an unforeseen event or condition, or a sudden or unexpected occasion for action and is beyond the control of the District.

7.4   No Change

7.5   No Change

7.6 Required Participation

Each member of the unit shall participate in the required Back-To-School and Open House nights, as well as participate in three (3) adjunct duties or ten (10) hours of adjunct duty (whichever comes first) related to student activities per year.

Examples of duties related to Student Activities are athletic events, club activities, dances, music, and drama events, and other social events. These adjunct duties shall be scheduled equitably among the members of the unit at each school site.

7.7   Activities/Assignments

Members of the unit shall participate in professional activities and perform professional assignments beyond the regular workday as needed and consistent with past practices of the District.

ARTICLE 8 LEAVES

8.1   No Change

8.2   No Change

8.3   No Change

8.4   No Change

8.5   No Change

8.6   Adoption & Child-Rearing Leave

A member of the unit (male or female) who wishes to take a personal leave to raise a child immediately following childbirth or upon adoption of a child, may be granted such leave without pay for up to one (1) year.

ARTICLE 9

Class Size

9.1   General

The following class sizes shall be defined as applicable for all schools in the District:

Grades: K   24
Grades 1–3   25
Grades 4–5   27
Grades 6–12   29 with the exception of science laboratories which shall have a maximum of 24 students.

9.2   Combination Classes

The class size for elementary classes, which combine one or more grade levels shall be reduced by one. The lower class size shall be used as the base for the reduction in class size.

9.3   Preparation time for middle and high school—No Change

9.4   300 Minutes of Preparation time every ten work days—No Change

9.5   Student Class Assignments

Student class assignments shall be made by the principal, or his/her designee. If student class assignments have been made by that would go over the class size limits stated in 9.1, the principal, or designee, shall follow the procedures below:

9.51 Combining Classes

Combination classes should be established by the principal if this procedure will bring the affected class(es) within the applicable maximum.

9.52 School Reassignment

The District administration may reassign students to other schools in the District is such a reassignment would bring the affected class(es) within the applicable maximum.

9.53 Other

When class sizes are exceeded or none of the procedures of 9.61 and 9.62 are feasible, the principal shall discuss the problem with the teachers of the affected classes and explore alternative approaches to resolve the problem.

ARTICLE 10

Transfer Procedure

10.1　Primary Consideration

The primary consideration in affecting assignments and transfers shall be to provide the best possible educational program for students and to assure that the needs of the school system will best be met.

10.2　General Principles

10.21　Transfer

A transfer is the movement of a unit member from one work location to another work location to another work location at a different work site.

10.22　Reassignment

A reassignment is the movement of a unit member from one subject area or grade level to another grade level at the same work site.

10.23　Basis

A transfer/reassignment shall not be made or denied arbitrarily, capriciously, or without a basis in fact.

10.3　Involuntary Transfer

10.31　The District shall seek volunteers prior to making any involuntary transfer/reassignment. If an involuntary transfer/reassignment becomes necessary, the unit member with the least District seniority shall be transferred or reassigned.

ARTICLE 12

Evaluation

12.1 Purpose

It is agreed and understood by the parties that the principal objective of the performance evaluation procedure is to maintain or improve the quality of education in the District.

12.12 Procedure

(a) Every probationary member of the unit shall be evaluated in writing by his/her immediate supervisor/principal in writing at least no later than February 15.

(b) Any member of the unit who receives a negative evaluation shall, upon request, be entitled to two (2) subsequent observations and a written evaluation of the observations. If the deficiency(ies) noted in the negative has been corrected, the second evaluation shall become part of the unit member's file, and shall be attached to the original evaluation.

(c) Hearsay shall not be included in a unit member's evaluation.

(d) A member of the unit shall have the right to have appended to an evaluation his/her response to the evaluation within twenty (20) school days of receipt of the evaluation. Such appended responses shall become part of the employee's personnel file. In all cases, the unit member shall be provided with copies of and all of her/his evaluations.

(e) The evaluation of members of the unit, except for alleged violation of procedural matters, shall not be subject to the Grievance Procedure.

12.2 Evaluation and Personnel Records

All materials, documents, and evidence used to form the evaluation/discipline of a unit member shall be open to inspection by the unit member. The unit member shall be notified in a timely fashion when materials, documents, evidence are placed in the unit member's personnel file that could be used for evaluation/discipline. The unit member shall have the right to timely append comments to such placed material, documents, and evidence.

DEBRIEFING

Please note, this debriefing memo was sent to the 22 members of my collective bargaining class. The class was broken into management and labor teams. The teams were further broken into Management A and Labor A which bargained together, and Management B and Labor B, which bargained together. Both A & B teams received the same information and the same letter of interest that guided their bargaining. The different teams underscored how personality impacts bargaining and its outcome. My graduate assistant, Martha Parker, and I traded off videotaping the bargaining sessions and observing the bargaining.

The debriefing memo sent to all members of the class follows.

DEBRIEFING SPRING 2009

Below are some questions and considerations that will help to focus our debriefing of the expedited bargaining sessions. Please review theses questions and be prepared to join the discussion that Martha (graduate assistant) and I will lead. Your bargaining was very interesting!!! Martha and I enjoyed watching you at work. We will review selected portions of the videotaping.

1. What surprised you at the table?
2. Were you prepared enough for bargaining? Was the other side prepared enough?
3. What were your takeaways from the simulation, what did you learn?
4. How did the use of technology influence, facilitate, or inhibit bargaining? What aspects worked the best? Once language was discussed at the table (supposals) and was typed into the applicable contract section and then appeared on the screen, was there a sense that the language had been agreed upon because it appeared on screen? Were you reluctant to change or challenge it once it was written for all to see?
5. Compare your contract with the Interest Letter that you received from your constituency. Did you meet or violate the interests? Management expanded leaves, why?
6. Labor came in with a complete package of all outstanding sections, how did that work? In their complete package, labor immediately gave on the burden sharing for fringe benefits (moved from 100 percent district paid to a percentage paid by the employee); did this concede a leverage point? Or, do you believe that it was important to setting a specific tone at the table?

7. Did you caucus too much, too little, or just right?
8. We did not see any water cooler negotiations. We wonder why?
9. How different was the second session of bargaining from the first? Why?
10. What role did personality play at the table?
11. Did you keep your constituency informed?
12. Did you find that you bargained with the other two parties, your team and your constituency?
13. Did you bring the principles of *Getting Together* and *Getting to Yes* to the table?
14. Did you develop an Elegant Solution?

AN ELEGANT SOLUTION FOR THE NEGOTIATED AGREEMENT

Richard Fossey, J.D., Ed.D.
Professor of Education Law
University of North Texas

Good faith bargaining hopefully leads to an "elegant" negotiation solution. An elegant solution includes:

1. The solution is better than any party's best alternative to a negotiated agreement.
2. All parties are committed to making the solution work.
3. The solution produces a good working relationship.
4. The solution is appropriate to long-term goals.
5. The solution can be feasibly implemented.
6. There is a clear understanding between the parties as to the meaning of the solution.
7. No joint interests are remaining to be addressed.
8. The process by which the agreement is achieved is seen by all parties as fair.

Appendix A-1   Arroyo Wells School District Age of Teachers

Age	Number	Age	Number
23	0	49	11
24	0	50	10
25	1	51	5
26	3	52	3
27	1	53	4
28	2	54	2
29	0	55	4
30	3	56	2
31	2	57	4
32	1	58	2
33	4	59	2
34	5	60	5
35	5	61	0
36	6	62	5
37	7	63	0
38	5	64	0
39	5	65	8
40	5	66	1
41	5	67	2
42	4	68	0
43	4	69	1
44	8		
45	7		
46	2		
47	12		
48	6	All ages are as of June 30th of this year	

Appendix A-2   Budget

Teacher Salary*	10,683,894
Teacher Stipends	387,500
Teacher Extra Duty	78,446
Administrator Salary*	1,020,312
Classified Salary	1,536,989
Total	13,707, 141
Teacher Benefits	3,902,269
Administrator Benefits	357,109
Classified Benefits	537,946
Total	4,797,324
Instructional Supplies	470,000
Books/Media	88,000
Total	558,000
Office Supplies	42,000
Transportation Maintenance	90,500
Transportation Supplies	78,500
Total	169,000
Utilities	1,105,000
Maintenance	682,500
TOTAL	**$21,060,965**

Appendix A-3   Comparative Pay Raises for Surrounding Districts

Year	Arroyo Wells	Metroville	Happy Valley
This Year			
Last Year	4.50%	4.25%	3.75%
Two Years	4.00%	3.75%	3.75%
Three Years	3.75%	3.50%	3.50%

FIVE-YEAR COMPARISON FOR EARLY
RETIREMENT INCENTIVE

School districts and other employers bargain early retirement packages as a means of cutting employee costs thus saving the school district money. It should not be approached as a reward for service. If that is the goal it is best to develop a specific reward program, which will likely be very difficult to do if it is linked to merit pay. Also, it is problematic to negotiate an ongoing retirement incentive that an employee can access any year. The school district must then negotiate an incentive on top of the incentive that it already gives.

Any incentive that management offers will more drastically reduce the total savings from the higher retiring teacher's salary compared to the lower, newly hired teacher's salary. Therefore, the district must find a balance between offering a large enough incentive to induce teachers to retire now rather than waiting for another year or two and making sure that the early retirement incentive plan does not cost the district more than it saves over five years. Management should approach early retirement incentive packages as a means to save money. The goal is to provide enough of an incentive for a teacher to decide to retire now rather than waiting. A teacher who was going to retire anyway does not save the district money; it costs the district because it is paying an incentive to do something the employee was going to do anyway.

A five-year comparison model provides the employer with information about how much of an incentive can be offered while meeting the goal of saving money. The comparison assumes no change in the current salary schedule. The replacement teacher is placed at the Step 1 BA and progresses each year for the following four years. The complete salary cost including fringe benefits is recalculated for each year for the Replacement Teacher. The cost difference between the Current Teacher and the Replacement is calculated for five years. It must be remembered that after conducting the five year comparison between the highest paid faculty member and the replacement costs for a new faculty member, the incentive must be subtracted from the five year comparison.

- Keeping the current teacher over five years, assuming no raises to the salary schedule, will cost the district $509,455
- Replacing the current teacher with a first year teacher, assuming no raises but movement down the salary schedule for each service, will cost the school district $298,453.
- The difference between keeping the current teacher and replacing that teacher over a five-year period is $211,002.

The employer can now find the cost for the incentive that it believes will yield the savings it desires.

Table A-4

Assumptions	Salary/Fringe
Current Teacher	
Step 11, M.A.+30	69,545
CAGS	1,000
Longevity 26+yrs	3,000
Retirement 5.8%	4,208
FICA 7.65%	5,550
Salary Total	83,303
Dental Single +1	744
Kaiser Single + 1	17,100
Disability Insurance	300
Life Insurance .21 per thousand salary	15 (73.545 X .21 = 15.44)
Worker's Comp. .54 per hundred	397 (735.45 X .54 = 397.14)
Unemployment	32
Fringe Benefit Total	$18,588
Grand Total	$101,891
Replacement Teacher—Year One	*Salary & Fringe*
Step 1, B.A.	34,121
Retirement 5.8%	1,979
FICA 7.65%	2,610
Salary Total	$38,710
Dental Single +1	744
Kaiser Single + 1	17,100
Disability Insurance	300
Life Insurance .21 per thousand salary	7 (34.121 X .21 = 7.17)
Worker's Comp. .54 per hundred	184 (341.21 X .54 = 184.25)
Unemployment	32
Fringe Benefit Total	$18,367
Grand Total	$57,077
Replacement Teacher—Year Two	*Salary & Fringe*
Step 2, B.A.	34,529
Retirement 5.8%	2,0003
FICA 7.65%	2,641
Salary Total	$39,173

(Continued)

Table A-4 *(Continued)*

Assumptions	Salary/Fringe
Dental Single +1	744
Kaiser Single + 1	17,100
Disability Insurance	300
Life Insurance .21 per thousand salary	7 (34.529 X .21 = 7.25)
Worker's Comp. .54 per hundred	186 (345.29 X .54 = 186.46)
Unemployment	32
Fringe Benefit Total	$18,369
Grand Total	$57,542
Replacement Teacher—Year Three	*Salary & Fringe*
Step 3, B.A.	36,119
Retirement 5.8%	2,095
FICA 7.65%	2,763
Salary Total	$40,977
Dental Single +1	744
Kaiser Single + 1	17,100
Disability Insurance	300
Life Insurance .21 per thousand salary	8 (36.119 X .21 = 7.58)
Worker's Comp. .54 per hundred	195 (361.19 X .54 = 195.04)
Unemployment	32
Fringe Benefit Total	$18,379
Grand Total	$59,356
Replacement Teacher—Year Four	*Salary & Fringe*
Step 4, B.A.	37,784
Retirement 5.8%	2,191
FICA 7.65%	2,890
Salary Total	$42,865
Dental Single +1	744
Kaiser Single + 1	17,100
Disability Insurance	300

(Continued)

Table A-4 *(Continued)*

Assumptions	Salary/Fringe
Life Insurance .21 per thousand salary	8 (37.784 X .21 = 7.93)
Worker's Comp. .54 per hundred	204 (377.84 X .54 = 204.03)
Unemployment	32
Fringe Benefit Total	$18,388
Grand Total	$61,253
Replacement Teacher—Year Five	*Salary & Fringe*
Step 5, B.A.	39,513
Retirement 5.8%	2,292
FICA 7.65%	3,023
Salary Total	$44,828
Dental Single +1	744
Kaiser Single + 1	17,100
Disability Insurance	300
Life Insurance .21 per thousand salary	8 (39.513 X .21 = 8.30)
Worker's Comp. .54 per hundred	213 (395.13 X .54 = 213.37)
Unemployment	32
Fringe Benefit Total	$18,397
Grand Total	$63,225

Savings over five years comparing current teacher with replacement teacher.

Year	Current Teacher Salary& Fringe	Replacement Salary & Fringe	Teacher Difference	YearlyTotal Difference
1	101,891	57,077	44,814	44,814
2	101,891	57,542	44,349	89,163
3	101,891	59,356	42,535	131,698
4	101,891	61,253	40,638	172,336
5	101,891	63,225	38,666	211,002

ARROYO WELLS SCHOOL DISTRICT FIVE-YEAR GRIEVANCE HISTORY

This AWSD grievance history tracks those grievances that reached Formal Level One. This history does not track those grievances either withdrawn or resolved at the informal level.

Table A.5

	Five Years Ago	
	Formal Level One	
Grievance Number	*Issue*	*Resolution*
#01–03	Placement on salary schedule	For employee
#02–03	Attendance at mandatory department meetings at high school (7.3 & 7.7)	Denied, past practice of requiring department meetings which are notfaculty meetings.
#03–03	Class size at elementary school (9.1)	Grievance withdrawn when a student moved out of the class
#04–03	Class size at elementary school (9.1)	Grievance withdrawn when a student moved out of the class
Formal Level Two-Superintendent		
#02–03	Attendance at mandatory department meetings at high school (7.3 & 7.7)	Denied, past practice of requiring department meetings which are not faculty meetings.
Formal Level Three-Advisory Arbitration		
#02–03	Attendance at mandatory department meetings at high school (7.3 & 7.7)	Arbitrator found for grievant citing 7.3
Formal Level Four-School Board		
#02–03	Attendance at mandatory department meetings at high school (7.3 & 7.7)	School board overturned arbitrator's decision stating that 7.7 and past practice were controlling, not 7.3

(Continued)

Table A.5 *(Continued)*

Four Years Ago

Formal Level One

Grievance Number	Issue	Resolution
#01–04	Involuntary reassignment form teaching four 8th grade history classes and one 7th grade history class to three 8th grade history classes and two 7th grade history classes (10.31)	Denied, reassignment not covered in section 10.31, past practice allows management to reassign teaching assignments within the building. NOTE: In the following year this contract section (10.31) was changed to add the word reassignment. The addition of the language did not reference this grievance.

Three Years Ago

No grievances were taken past the informal level.

Two Years Ago

Formal Level One

#01–05	Content of the evaluation (12.12b)	Denied, cannot grieve the content of an evaluation. All procedures of 12.12 were followed. 12.12(e) is controlling.
#02–05	Derogatory letter from parents was placed in the employee's personnel file without reasonable notice and was used in an evaluation (12.2)	Denied, citing 12.12(c) that letter was not hearsay and 12.12 (e) can't grieve substance of evaluation.

Formal Level Two-Superintendent

#02–05	Derogatory letter from parents was placed in the employee's personnel file without reasonable notice and was used in an evaluation (12.2)	Denied, citing 12.12(c) that letter was not hearsay and 12.12 (e) can't grieve substance of evaluation.

(Continued)

Table A.5   *(Continued)*

Grievance Number	Issue	Resolution
Formal Level Three-Advisory Arbitration		
#02–05	Derogatory letter from parents was placed in the employee's personnel file without reasonable notice and was used in an evaluation (12.2)	Accepted, citing that employee did not receive timely notice of the derogatory letter from parents in a reasonable or timely manner. Therefore, the employee never had the opportunity to provide a response. 12.2 controlling, content of evaluation must only use information appropriately gathered.
Formal Level Four-School Board		
#02–05	Derogatory letter from parents was placed in the employee's personnel file without reasonable notice and was used in an evaluation (12.2)	Accepted arbitrator's decision. Derogatory letter expunged and evaluation withdrawn. Evaluation must be rewritten without the use of derogatory letter.
	Last Year	
Formal Level One		
#01–06	Class size at elementary school (9.1)	Withdrawn when a student left the classroom.
#02–06	Class size at elementary school (9.1)	Denied citing 9.63, exploring possible alternatives
#03–06	Class size at elementary school (9.1)	Withdrawn when a student left the classroom
#04–06	Faculty meeting at high school went fifteen minutes over the one hour limit (7.3)	Denied. Faculty meeting started fifteen minutes late because faculty came to the meeting late.
#05–06	Class size at elementary school (9.1)	Denied citing 9.63, exploring possible alternatives

(Continued)

Table A.5 *(Continued)*

Formal Level Two-Superintendent

Grievance Number	Issue	Resolution
#02–06	Class size at elementary school (9.1)	Resolved when additional students moved into school, which resulted in establishment of a combination grade.
#05–06	Class size at elementary school (9.1)	Denied but was later withdrawn before advisory arbitration hearing

Table A.6

	Current Fringe Benefit Costs for Teachers Current School Year Monthly Costs (employees in plan)		
Plan	*Single*	*Single +1*	*Family*
Dental	32 (34)	67 (62)	110 (79)
Kaiser S	713 (8)	1,425 (22)	1,925 (32)
Blue Cross	755 (14)	1,511 (31)	2,040 (44)
IPM	668 (4)	1,336 (9)	1,804 (11)

Current plans do not have a co-pay option.

Monthly and Total Costs by Plan

Plan	*Single*	*Single +1*	*Family*	*Yearly Total*
Dental	1,088	4,154	8,690	$167,184
Kaiser S	5,704	31,350	61,600	$1,183,848
Blue Cross	10,570	46,841	89,760	$1,766,052
IPM	2,672	12,024	19,844	$414,480
Total Costs				$3,531,564

Fringe Benefit Monthly Costs with a $10 Co-Pay

Plan	*Single*	*Single +1*	*Family*
Dental No Co-Pay Option Available Under Current Plan			
Kaiser S	670	1,339	1,810
Blue Cross	709	1,420	1,917
IPM	627	1,255	1,695

GRIEVANCE FORM

Grievance Number_____

Name of Grievant_____ Date Filed _____

AWSD/AWTA Contract Years_____

Alleged Violation of Section_____

Briefly explain how this section of the contract was violated, misapplied, or misinterpreted.

_____

_____

_____

_____

Date of Alleged Violation

_____

Proposed Remedy

_____

_____

_____

Informal Level Response from District

_____

_____

_____

Date Informal Level Meeting Held

_____

Participants in the Informal Level Meeting

_____

_____

_____   _____

Name of Person Receiving the Grievance   Date

ALL RESPONSES FROM THIS POINT ON MUST BE MADE IN WRITING AND APPENDED TO THIS GRIEVANCE FORM. THIS INCLUDES DISTRICT RESPONSES, AND EMPLOYEE/UNION RESPONSES AND REQUESTS TO MOVE THE GRIEVANCE TO THE NEXT LEVEL IF THE RESPONSE IS UNSATISFACTORY. TIMELINES WILL BE ADHERED TO BY ALL PARTIES. REQUESTS FOR ARBITRATION MUST BE SIGNED BY THE ASSOCIATION PRESIDENT.

GRIEVANCE LOG AWTA

_____**Grievance Number**

Informal Level Outcome

_____Date Grievance Accepted

_____Date Grievance Denied

_____Date Grievance Appealed to Next Level

Formal Level One

_____Date Grievance Accepted

_____Date Grievance Denied

_____Date Grievance Appealed to Next Level

Formal Level Two

_____Date Grievance Accepted

_____Date Grievance Denied

_____Date Grievance Appealed to Next Level

Formal Level Three

_____Date Grievance Accepted

_____Date Grievance Denied

_____Date Grievance Appealed to Next Level

_____**Grievance Number**

Informal Level Outcome

_____Grievance Accepted

_____Grievance Denied

_____Grievance Appealed to Next Level

Formal Level One
_____Date Grievance Accepted
_____Date Grievance Denied
_____Date Grievance Appealed to Next Level

Formal Level Two

_____Date Grievance Accepted

_____Date Grievance Denied

_____Date Grievance Appealed to Next Level

Formal Level Three

_____Date Grievance Accepted

_____Date Grievance Denied

_____Date Grievance Appealed to Next Level

Table A-7   Metroville School District

			Salary Schedule		
Step/Year	BA	BA+15	MA/BA+45	MA+15	MA+30
1	34,806	36,242	39,286	40,901	42,581
2	35,354	36,791	39,835	41,450	43,130
3	35,903	37,339	40,383	41,998	43,678
4	37,661	39,167	42,362	44,057	45,819
5	39,505	41,087	44,439	46,216	48,065
6	41,441	43,099	46,614	48,478	50,416
7	43,471	45,210	48,897	50,852	52,887
8	45,601	47,424	51,292	53,342	55,477
9	47,835	49,748	53,805	55,958	58,195
10	50,178	52,183	56,441	58,698	61,047
11	52,635	54,741	59,205	61,573	64,037
12		58,533	63,172	65,632	68,258

Source: Education Stipend—Added to the Salary Base
Ed.D./Ph.D. = $4,000

Longevity Stipend—Added to the Base But Not Cumulative
13 years of continuous service in the district = $500
14 to 15 years of continuous service in the district = $1,000
16 to 17 years of continuous service in the district = $1,250
18 to 19 years of continuous service in the district = $1,500
20 to 29 years of continuous service in the district = $2,000
30 + years of continuous service in the district = $3,00

Table A-8   Data on Teachers Age 55 and Older

36 teachers are currently age 55 or older with at least ten years of service in the AWSD
Number of teachers with a CAGS degree—6
Number of teachers with an Ed.D./Ph.D.—3

Distribution of teachers by health plan.

Plan	Single	Single+1	Family
Dental	6	27	3
Kaiser (an HMO)	1	9	1
Blue Cross	4	18	2
IPM	1	0	0

Distribution on the salary schedule.

Age	MA	MA+15	MA+30
55	1		3
56			2
57	1	1	2
58			2
59		1	1
60			5
61			
62		2	3
63			
64			
65		2	6
66		1	
67			2
68			
69			1

Table A.9   Scattergram: Arroyo Wells School District

Year	BA	BA+15	MA	MA +15	MA+30	Total
1	1					1
2		2				2
3	1	1				2
4	1	1				2
5	1	1				2
6		3				3
7	2	2	2			6
8		1	1			2
9		5	5	5		15
10		25	22	15		62
11					78	78
Total	6	41	30	20	78	175

B.A. = $234,121
B.A.+15 = $2,043,401
MA = $1,730,332
MA+15 = $1,251530
MA+30 = $5,424,510
TOTAL Salary = $10,683894

Stipend for each degree held
CAGS—$1,500 stipend added to salary each year X 18 = $27,000
Ed.D/Ph.D.—$2,500 stipend added to salary each year X 7 = $17,500

Longevity Stipend—Added to Base Salary and Education Stipend—Non-Cumulative
12 to 13 years of continuous service in AWSD = $750 X 14 = $10,500
14 to 16 years of continuous service in AWSD = $1,500 X 16 = $24,000
17 to 19 years of continuous service in AWSD = $2,000 X 17 = 34,000
20 to 25 years of continuous service in AWSD = $2,500 X 27 = $67,500
26 + years of continuous service in AWSD = $3,000 X 69 = $207,000
TOTAL Stipends = $387,500

GRAND TOTAL FROM SALARY SCHEDULE = $11,071,394

Table A-10

	Arroyo Wells School District Teacher Seniority List Years of Service		
Year	*# of Teachers*	*Year*	*# of Teachers*
2008-	1	1983-	6
2007	2	1982-	10
2006-	2	1981-	8
2005-	2	1980-	9
2004-	2	1979-	5
2003	3	1978-	3
2002	4	1977-	4
2001-	1	1976-	1
2000	6	1975-	1
1999-	4	1974-	4
1998-	5	1973-	3
1997-	6	1972-	0
1996-	8	1971-	2
1995-	7	1970-	0
1994-	4	1969-	5
1993-	5	1968-	4
1992-	5	1967-	1
1991-	8	1966-	2
1990-	4	1965-	0
1989-	3	1964-	1
1988-	7		
1987-	5		
1986-	4		
1985-	5		
1984-	3		

Table A-11 Happy Valley School District

Years/Step	BA	BA+15	BA+30	MA	MA+15	MA+30
			Salary Schedule			
1	32,009	33,774	35,540	37,307	39,072	40,839
2	33,665	35,430	37,196	38,963	40,728	42,495
3	35,321	37,086	38,852	40,619	42,384	44,151
4	36,977	38,742	40,508	42,275	44,040	45,807
5	38,633	40,398	42,164	43,931	45,696	47,463
6	40,289	42,054	43,820	45,587	47,352	49,119
7	41,945	43,710	45,476	47,243	49,008	50,775
8	43,602	45,366	47,132	48,899	50,664	52,431
9	45,256	47,022	48,788	50,555	52,320	54,087
10	46,912	48,678	50,444	52,210	53,976	55,743
11				53,865	55,632	57,399
12				55,423	57,288	59,055
13				57,181	58,944	60,711

Source: Longevity Stipend—The stipends are not cumulative
14–16 years of continuous service = $500
17–19 years of continuous service = $1,000
20–22 years of continuous service = $1,500
23+ years of continuous service = $2,000

SICK LEAVE

The certificated teaching staff earns one day of sick leave per month up to 10 months per year (10 sick leave days per year maximum). Each person may accumulate up to a maximum of 120 days of sick leave. Upon separation, after five consecutive years of service in the district, the certificated staff member shall be reimbursed for any earned but unused days of sick leave up to the maximum of 120 days at 50 percent of his/her per diem salary as per the existing salary schedule. Extra-curricular, summer school, special extra-duty hourly wages, and/or special project payments shall not be computed in the per diem salary computation for reimbursement of unused sick leave days.

Appendix B

Only members of the District Bargaining Team should read this memo

TO: District Bargaining Team
FR: Arroyo Wells School District Superintendent
RE: Bargaining Interests

As you prepare for our 10 hours of expedited bargaining in an effort to settle the contract I want to share with you the interests that you are to pursue at the bargaining table. We have five major interests.

First, because of budget concerns we must hold the line on increasing our ongoing expenditures. Proposals that increase ongoing salary commitments beyond where we currently are in negotiations and without a short term or long term improvement in the budget must be avoided.

- Class size is a salary issue as well as an instructional issue. If we lower class size we will incur more costs not just for the addition of the teacher but at the elementary school level to support the 300 minutes of release time every ten school days. We will have to add additional faculty as we increase the number of elementary school teachers. We are not seeking to change the 300 minutes of preparation time for elementary school teachers. However, if we can reduce the number of students from two to one for Section 9.2 combination classes that will assist our cost cutting as well. We need to explore options about what to do when we cannot reduce the size of a class when it violates the class size section of the contract. We need flexibility.
- Salary increases must be held down. Any offer above the one percent on the table must show cost savings in other areas—fringe benefits, class size, early retirement are possible cost saving measures. Paid leaves and

197

changes to the extra duty stipend also impact the salary budget line. If you increase the salary budget line, you must demonstrate a savings in some other budget line. It is in our best interest to show the full cost of a teacher. The format for calculating early retirement is very useful.

Second, we need to move from the 100% paid benefits. This has long-term disastrous consequences for the budget. The more money that we pour into premium costs reduces the amount of money available for other competing demands including salary. It is in our best interests, and I believe the best interests of our teachers to get a handle on these escalating costs through some form of burden sharing. Either a dollar cap on benefits that the district pays or a percentage sharing plan will meet our interests.

Because this is such an important issue we will probably need to make sure that the teachers are held harmless with no increase for at least one year, maybe two at the most. One way to do that is to raise the cap to a level that no individual teacher will have any out-of-pocket expenses for at least one or two years. If you bargain a percentage you can look at an off the salary schedule mitigation for one year or two years maximum. This mitigation would involve a set dollar amount that equals the differential between the 100 percent and the reduced percentage the district pays. This amount would not go on the salary schedule and would be issued as a one-time bonus.

Three, we need to change 10.3. The word reassignment must come out. We need the flexibility to reassign teachers within a building without this convoluted movement necessitated by bumping through the schools based on district seniority. While this is very important to us, I am concerned about setting a precedent in which we trade language for money.

Four, an early retirement package would be nice and would serve our interests only if we can show that it saved the district money over a five year period.

Five, we can no longer hold on to advisory arbitration. According to PELRB decisions (and consistent with federal National Labor Relations Board decisions) a workable grievance process must end in binding arbitration. If the grievance procedure does not, PELRB will allow an advisory arbitration grievance to be elevated to an unfair labor practice. Either way, a third party neutral, the arbitrator or the PELRB, will render a binding decision on the school board. See what you can get for it.

Six, Section 7.7 is one that the AWTA wants to change. It has worked well for us. It gives us flexibility. It is very important that we keep this flexibility. Without it we may find ourselves in a situation in which every activity that has not been spelled out explicitly in the contract results in a change in past practice and an occasion to renegotiate additional stipends and hourly rates. This is important.

You represent the school district, its community, and the students. Be willing to play hardball if called for. But, also remember we must work with the teachers after bargaining. We do not want bargaining to resemble General Sherman's march to Atlanta, we win but destroy everything in our path. The teachers are our colleagues and not an enemy or an obstacle. Please keep me up to date after each meeting. If you are concerned that a specific proposal may violate our interests, you must talk to me right away.

Best wishes on your bargaining.

Appendix C

Only members of the AWTA Bargaining Team should read this memo

TO: AWTA Bargaining Team
FR: Todd DeMitchell, President
RE: Expedited Bargaining

I know that you have begun the process of preparing for our two-day expedited bargaining sessions in an effort to settle the contract or declare impasse. I want to restate our interests as you continue your preparations. Our interests should guide your actions at the Table. If you are unclear about any proposals potentially running counter to our interests, please contact me right away. I am also available should you need information or want to discuss strategies.

Salary is an obvious interest of ours. We want to be paid the best wage that we can given the important and vital professional service that we render to the community. We must also be realistic as to the reasonableness of our salary demands. We want a competitive wage that attracts new teachers and retains experienced teachers.

The maintenance of needed fringe benefits is important. Unfortunately, we are facing a dilemma. The costs of fringe benefits are escalating at an alarming rate and have been doing so for a number of years. This is a challenge not only for the district, but for us as well. We have reached the point where the new available monies going into the maintenance of our extraordinary benefit package—which, by the way, we are quite proud of the fact that we have negotiated a package that is the envy of surrounding school districts—is starting to erode the salary increases.

It is in our best interests not to let the balance of salary and benefits shift too far out of balance. We can posture publicly as much as we want about how the district must pay for both and that the costs of increased insurance premiums should not be placed on the backs of hardworking teachers. However, the Association leadership is concerned that the reality of financing public schools and the uncontrolled costs of rising medical and dental insurance has forced us into a position that 100% district paid for benefits may no longer be sustainable. If necessary, explore options that mitigate the impact of this potential burden shifting. If we give something on fringe we need to get something in return that we can sell to our constituency. If you can gain an additional year or two before implementation of a cost-sharing proposal that would serve our members in the short run and provide for a better balance in the long run.

We want to enhance our professional status, if possible. We look at professionalism as having more control over our time and manageable class size. Even if the research does not support a small reduction in class size, we definitely do not want an increase.

Related to professional status is section 7.7 on professional responsibilities. This has been a thorn in our side even though management has been circumspect in its use. It could, however, expand and place more control over our time in the hands of management. Try to get a modification of the language limiting its reach. It is important that we get our position on the Table for future negotiations. We must continue to push against this even though not getting a change is not a deal breaker for us. Failure to get a change does not trigger a BATNA (Best Alternative to a Negotiated Agreement).

The issue of reassignment can be a troubling one for us. If we sacrifice flexibility for a rigid seniority of reassignments we will bounce our members through the schools. This is a battle that we don't want to take on because it would be a battle within our membership. We can defend seniority as a basis for transfers but it is a less potent argument in face of large movements of teachers. If we can get the district to buy into the notion of school level seniority it may be more palatable for our members. This is something the district wants, use it trade for something we want.

Binding arbitration is a big deal. The members want the sense of fairness that comes with binding arbitration. Similarly, the ability to grieve the content of an observation and or evaluation would be a great win. However, it is not so important that we would sacrifice other important interests.

A number of our more senior members are clamoring for an early retirement package. It is in our best interests to get the best deal that we can.

These interests should guide your actions at the Table. It is important that you keep me apprised as to your progress.

Solidarity!

About the Author

Todd A. DeMitchell has represented two school districts in California at the bargaining table. In addition, he has consulted with school boards on bargaining and with school administrators as well as teachers on grievances, unfair labor practices, and managing the contract. DeMitchell spent eighteen years in the public schools of California as a substitute teacher, elementary school teacher, assistant principal, principal, director of personnel and labor relations, and superintendent. He studied collective bargaining at the University of Southern California (Ed.D.) and at Harvard University (postdoctorate). He is currently the chair of the Department of Education and a professor in the Department of Education and in the Justice Studies Program at the University of New Hampshire. He also served as an associate professor and department chair at Sonoma State University. This is his fifth book and the third one published by Rowman & Littlefield Education. His other books include *Negligence: What Principals Need to Know to Avoid Liability* and *The Limits of Law-Based School Reform: Vain Hopes and False Promises*, with Richard Fossey. He has published over 135 book chapters and articles in peer-reviewed journals, law reviews, and professional journals. His research and teaching interests are school law and labor relations.

Made in the USA
Lexington, KY
22 October 2014